For all Mankind

A book about the Old Testament and about us

To the people of St. George's, Jerusalem
and to our other friends,
Christian, Jewish and Muslim
in that terrible and beautiful land

Stuart Blanch Archbishop of York

Deolan
1976

For all Mankind

A book about the Old Testament
and about us

The Bible Reading Fellowship

St. Michael's House, 2 Elizabeth Street, London SW1W 9RQ

Contents

Author's Introduction

Author's Introduction

This little book is not intended for scholars and theologians, or for those who aspire to be such. If any such should happen upon it, they will have to forgive the unsupported assertions and sweeping generalisations with which it abounds. Neither is it intended to be a compendium of Old Testament knowledge. This is already well provided for in dictionaries and commentaries. It is intended for those who find the Old Testament a jungle of chaotic ideas, unfinished themes and tangled history and are looking for a route through it. It goes without saying that the route I have suggested is not the only possible one but it offers certain vantage points and perspectives which may be helpful.

The Old Testament is a book for mankind, not just for theologians, philosophers or antiquarians. It is a book which is meant to throw some light on our path, to put a spring in our step and a song in our hearts. This it has done down the centuries without the benefit of exact scholarship or profound learning. Thank God for that. But the Old Testament is not concerned just with the individual believer; it expresses the mind of God for communities and nations; it is a book for all mankind – not just for Hebrew or Christian mankind, western or middle class mankind – and in the troubled conditions of the twentieth century we could do worse than return to this ancient source of experience and wisdom. So in your search for truth, however pursued, may God, if necessary, deny you peace but give you glory.

However simple an author may try to be, the fact remains that the Old Testament is a book of great complexity and the reader will have to exercise some patience in his approach to it. In this respect the four appendices at the end of the book are of more than usual importance and it would be sensible to make yourself familiar with them before you begin. The questions which are provided may be used either as the basis for group discussion or as a means of keeping alert to the main issues. You could glance at them before you start and perhaps turn to them again at the beginning of the chapter to which they relate.

Finally, may I acknowledge my indebtedness, conscious and unconscious, to many other students of the Old Testament – and in particular to Ian Thomson, Director of the Bible Reading Fellowship, who encouraged me to attempt this book, to my Secretary at Liverpool, Miss Pamela Edis who painstakingly typed the manuscript and to my wife by whom you have been saved from many needless obscurities.

STUART EBOR:

Bishopthorpe,
York

ACKNOWLEDGEMENTS

Appendices 3 and 4 owe much to the following books, which are both helpful aids:
Samuel Sandmel, *The Enjoyment of Scripture*, Oxford University Press 1972;
Encyclopaedia of Dates and Events, English University Press 1968.

design/print Eyre & Spottiswoode Ltd, Thanet Press

1 A library in your hand
Many authors – one message

The Old Testament is a very complex book. It was written,
collected and handed on over a period of fifteen hundred
years until it reached the form in which we are familiar
with it in the first century of the Christian era. It comes
from many hands, and it comprises many different types
of literature – poetry and prose, narration and oration,
shopping lists and inventories, family trees and court
records, proverbs and prophecies. You have a library in
your hand. And this makes it all the more remarkable that
the theme of the Bible can be summed up in four
monosyllabic words: 'The Lord is King'. This is very
remarkable because most of the writers of the Bible were
unaware of what their fellow writers had written –
inevitably so, since the writings circulated for years and
even centuries before they achieved any collective form.
Isaiah, as far as we are aware, never met Hosea; Moses
never met Abraham; David never met Deborah. Moreover
the writers had very different purposes in mind. Some
were rather pedantic court scribes, not too scrupulous
about the exact truth but eager to please their patrons.
Some were poets; some were honest narrators of events as
they saw them; some wrote with philosophical or apologetic
intent. Some of them wrote, just because they liked writing.
Yet it would be no exaggeration to say that from every
one of these books emerges, by word or implication, the
deeply held conviction of the Hebrew people that the
Lord (their Lord) is King.

This conviction, of course, took many different forms.
Sometimes it was little more than an expression of
nationalist feeling – the notion that God was on their side
and therefore they could look for victory over their
enemies. But at the other end of the spectrum it could
take the form of an astonishing belief that their particular
Lord was not only their King but King of all the earth
and King of the universe as well. When you consider that
these writers lived under conditions not that much
dissimilar from our own, with wars and rumours of wars,
profiteering and inflation, economic disorders and

unemployment, and the simple but dread facts of sickness, senility and death, the belief that there is a Lord who is King of all the earth and controls it with love and mercy is an astonishing one – so astonishing that subsequent theologians have had to give to that particular belief the status of a 'revelation'. It is not something which would occur to you when you were lying in bed with the toothache or wondering where the next meal was coming from or trying to cope with a teenage family. Yet this is the message which breaks the surface at some point in every book of the Old Testament. It is important, therefore, as you read it to bear this theme in mind and observe the mysterious way in which it emerges in many guises and under varying forms.

May I change the analogy from the library in your hand to the symphony on your record player? The basic theme of many a symphony is simple. The composer's skill consists in the ability to express and re-express this theme in a great variety of modes, using a whole range of orchestration to impart its message, giving that theme a profundity and a relevance which it could not possibly have when played on a penny whistle. My task therefore will be, having enunciated the theme, to try to demonstrate how that theme is handled by a variety of persons under a variety of circumstances, and to show how that theme is as relevant to us in the twentieth century after Christ as it was to our forefathers in the twentieth century before Christ, as relevant to the Third World as to ourselves of the West, as relevant to communist societies as to capitalist ones. The Bible is not just a book of private devotion, nor the peculiar property of a peculiar people, nor a source from which to draw texts for sermons, nor a book for reading from brass eagles in mediaeval churches – but a book for all mankind. I do not pretend that this is an easy task, but it is worth persevering with if it leads to a way of life somewhat more creative and dynamic than the one to which we have grown accustomed.

2 Madness in my method
A guide to the reader

It would have been possible to write this book as a solemn academic exercise of the kind to which a candidate for some Honours School of Theology is subjected. There would have been a long introductory chapter about the nature of the documents comprising the Old Testament, a description of the process by which the documents reached their present form and how they were collected into the three parts of the so-called Hebrew Canon. There would then have been a long section on the first Canon (the *Torah* or Teaching or Pentateuch as we variously call it); an even longer section on the Prophets divided into the Former Prophets (what we call the historical books) and the Latter Prophets; and then a third section on the Writings, a miscellany dating on the whole from the latter part of the pre-Christian era (see Appendix 2). The book would have ended with a triumphant summary, which would no doubt have been extremely interesting to the reader if he had had the patience to go that far. This is precisely the problem about the Old Testament. For a proper appreciation, it requires a considerable body of technical knowledge which the professional may rightly be expected to acquire but can hardly be expected of the amateur, who simply wants to know what the Old Testament has to say to him and to the society in which he lives.

Yet some guidance is necessary, as for any ancient literature, and I became vividly aware of this when I began to read the Bible myself seriously for the first time. Because it is normal to read in this way, I started to read at the beginning in the fond hope of getting through to the end. All went well for the book of Genesis because the issues it handles are sufficiently profound and universal to command the attention of any human being who is interested in them. But you will not be surprised to learn that my programme of reading came to a grinding halt about a third of the way through the book of Leviticus. If I had started with the Prophets I would have been in no better case. It is like attempting a concerto before you can

master the scales, or a full-length oil painting before you
have learnt to draw. That is why so many people fall back
baffled before this ancient literature or content themselves
with using it as a quarry from which they dig useful
devotional lessons or texts to hurl at their adversaries.
Hence the method I propose to use. I shall attempt a
series of graded 'lessons', interesting enough, I hope, to
command the interest of the willing reader but not so
complicated in the early stages as to discourage him
altogether. Technical matters will be dealt with not in a
great indigestible mass at the beginning of the book but as
they actually arise out of the text. You will not be reading
the Bible either in chronological order or in date-of-
authorship order. You will be attending to the simpler
issues first, and only later to the more complex ones.
What I hope, however, will emerge is a conspectus of the
Old Testament literature which will enable you, on the
principles you have learned, to handle any part of that
literature with reasonable confidence that you are being
true to the author's intention and are sufficiently aware of
the textual and theological problems involved. It goes
without saying that this exercise will be useless without
continuing attention to the text itself. Almost any
translation will do, provided you have an alternative at
your elbow (see Appendix 1). But you will need to be
aware that the differences you observe in the English text
from one Bible to another are not due simply to the whims
of the translator but to a gradual perfecting of the original
text – a long and highly skilled process which has been
going on now for many centuries. There are no 'autograph
documents' available to us. By that is meant that we do
not have in our possession any of the documents of the
Bible as they were originally written. We have only copies
and versions; it has been the task of the textual critic
over the years to make judgements between these copies,
and thereby to choose that version of the text which in his
view is nearest to the original. You will also need to be
aware that the task of the translator is not primarily to
make the Bible sound attractive or convincing, but to
provide you with what the original author either wrote or
said – and that is often obscure, sometimes clumsy and
inevitably inadequate to the great theme which the divine
Author himself has in mind. I hope, therefore, that you
will find that there is method in my madness after all.

3

Scepticism, ancient and modern
Ecclesiastes

When I first suggested to a friend that I might begin this
study of the Old Testament with the Book of Ecclesiastes
I was rewarded with expressions of astonishment and
disbelief. Most people have never read it and only a few
will know where it is to be found in the Bible. The only
really familiar section of it is chapter 12 which is occasionally
read on solemn occasions in church when the vicar is
looking for a suitably sonorous passage to come before
the Magnificat, or at a school prizegiving when the
headmaster is looking for something which will not be
too offensive to parents of diverse faith or of no faith at all.
So here it is in the rotund but largely impenetrable language
of the Authorised Version: 'Remember now thy Creator
in the days of thy youth, while the evil days come not, nor
the years draw nigh, when thou shalt say, I have no
pleasure in them; While the sun, or the light, or the moon,
or the stars, be not darkened, nor the clouds return after
the rain: In the day when the keepers of the house shall
tremble, and the strong men shall bow themselves, and the
grinders cease because they are few, and those that look
out of the windows be darkened, And the doors shall be
shut in the streets, when the sound of the grinding is low,
and he shall rise up at the voice of the bird, and all the
daughters of musick shall be brought low; Also when they
shall be afraid of that which is high, and fears shall be in the
way, and the almond tree shall flourish, and the grasshopper
shall be a burden, and desire shall fail: because man goeth
to his long home, and the mourners go about the streets:
Or ever the silver cord be loosed, or the golden bowl
be broken, or the pitcher be broken at the fountain, or the
wheel broken at the cistern. Then shall the dust return to
the earth as it was: and the spirit shall return unto God
who gave it. Vanity of vanities, saith the preacher; all is
vanity.' (12:1–8)

Why then choose this little known and rather inconsequential
book? I choose it for two reasons, which follow naturally
from my comments in the previous chapter. The first is
that for all the textual difficulties which will be encountered

in it, it is the kind of book which can be read and be made sense of in almost any place, in almost any period of history and by any kind of person. It is not the product of a sect but a cry from humanity as a whole. The second reason is that it illustrates certain basic facts of which any reader of the Bible needs to be aware almost as soon as he begins to read it. Let me elaborate.

I mentioned in the previous chapter that there are three 'Canons' of Scripture in the Hebrew Bible (page 3; see Appendix 2). This needs to be understood if we are to approach the Old Testament without doing violence to the intentions of the authors or of the collectors. The Bible you will have in your hand, unless you are a Hebrew scholar (and I apologise to such if there are any), will be the Bible based upon the order of books in the Vulgate (the Latin translation) and upon its predecessor (the Greek translation) called the Septuagint. The Septuagint was designed for Greek-speaking Jews and Gentiles in Alexandria and elsewhere in the Mediterranean, and it was felt necessary to put the books in what the translators felt to be a more rational order than the original Hebrew Bible. The Pentateuch retained its place of honour at the beginning of the book. Then the histories were gathered together – Joshua, Judges, 1/2 Samuel, 1/2 Kings, 1/2 Chronicles, Ezra and Nehemiah – because they seemed to provide a history of the Jewish people. Then came the Prophets, more or less as we have them now, and then the other documents were dispersed rather arbitrarily where they seemed best to fit. We shall need to escape from the strait-jacket of this order if we are to understand the basis of the original Hebrew Bible, which was divided into three Canons largely based upon the date or imputed date of the books. The first Canon is the *Torah*, so-called in the Hebrew Bible, which for the Hebrew scholar is the 'holy of holies'. It is the 'Teaching' which is seen to underlie all Hebrew life, thought and culture. The second Canon was composed of the Former Prophets which (oddly enough to our ears) include 1/2 Samuel and 1/2 Kings, and the Latter Prophets which include all that we understand by the Prophets in our Bible, excluding the book of Daniel. Well, you may say, this is very odd because of all the prophetic books surely Daniel is the most 'prophetic'. The fact of the matter, however, is that the book of Daniel was evidently thought to come from the latter part of the pre-Christian era and therefore could only be consigned to the third Canon, i.e. the Writings, which enjoyed a status something akin to the status which the Apocrypha now enjoys in the Protestant Churches – not to be treated as a basis for doctrine but interesting and in varying degrees edifying. So now we have placed the book of Ecclesiastes in context. It is part of the Writings and even its place there was often disputed by the Rabbis because of what was regarded as its extreme scepticism. That at least should encourage twentieth-century Western man to read it.

The book Ecclesiastes also illustrates three other points with which we shall have to grow familiar in the course of our studies. The first is that it purports to be from the hand of Solomon ('I was King in Jerusalem' ch. 1:12) – but this is a literary convention of the day which saw Moses as the fountainhead of all law, David as the fountainhead of all psalmody and Solomon as the fountainhead of all wisdom. Most scholars would now agree that the book dates from the so-called Greek period in which the Hebrew nation was being exposed to the dangerous intellectual solvents of Hellenism and was having to fight to maintain its ancient faith. So whilst it should appeal to the twentieth-century sceptic, who finds religious faith increasingly irrelevant, it should also appeal to the twentieth-century churchman trying to get his feet on to some firm rock with the sea of doubt washing around him. The second point would not be obvious to you if you are a regular churchgoer and hear the lessons read Sunday after Sunday in the same kind of ecclesiastical voice. In the Old Testament we are dealing with a literature of amazing variety and range. We do not, for example, read an article from the Daily Express in the same way as a Shakespearian tragedy. We do not read a couplet from Omar Khayyam in the way we recite a limerick. And yet this is precisely what we often do when we read the Old Testament, thus giving it a totally misleading uniformity, as if the literature were all of one piece, in one style, with the same emotional tone throughout. The third point is that we must be true to the author's intention, and nowhere is this more important than in the book of Ecclesiastes. Learned men have sifted through this book during the years and sometimes discovered as many as eleven or twelve authors in it

because of the seeming inconsistencies within the document
and the varieties of emotional tone betrayed in it. We must
therefore go back and ask the basic question, 'What kind
of document is it?' The Hebrew title (*Qoheleth*) could mean
'The Preacher', in which case we are in the presence of a
sermon, and, some of you will say, a typically dreary
sermon at that, with no beginning and no end and not
much middle. Or is it just a philosophical dissertation?
Or is it a treatise for a D.Phil. in a university of the
ancient world? Or is it a tract designed for distribution
outside a gymnasium in Alexandria? The value of the
book will entirely depend upon the answer you give to
this question. You must learn to ask this question of every
book in the Bible which you read, whether it is 1/2 Samuel
or Daniel, or Ezra or Genesis.

At this point I ought to leave you to get on with it and
perhaps write the answer upside down at the end of the
book. I will, however, offer a suggestion. If the ancient
world had its five-year diaries this would be one of them.
That is why it sounds so inconsistent. One day the author
is full of faith, the next day full of doubt; one day in love
with his wife, the next day out of love with her; one day
in robust health enjoying his pleasures like any latter-day
hedonist, the next day with a pain in his chest wondering
what is going to happen to him. He writes as he feels.
It is the book of a busy executive who has had a marked
degree of success and is now beginning to wonder what it
all adds up to. It is the book of a busy minister of the
gospel who has just resigned from his last parish and is
wondering whether the faith he has so patiently expounded
to others is going to be of any avail to himself. It is the
book of an international statesman who looks back along
the corridors of power and wonders whether his journeys
were really necessary. It is the book of any King in any
Jerusalem, who looks out across the human scene, with a
lifetime of experience behind him, and dares to believe
that it was all vanity. I say 'dares to believe' because this
is an extremely daring book, facing up to issues which most
of us would choose to disregard and facing up to them
with impeccable honesty and not dodging the answers. So
I return to my original point – this is a book for all
mankind; Jew or Gentile, Hindu or Christian, Muslim or
atheist; it can be read and understood with the minimum
of technical knowledge. So read chapter 12 again, this

time in your own version or, if you have it, in the New English Bible. It is the cry of every man as he views the dread prospects of declining powers, senility, death and annihilation. You will not feel any better for reading this remarkable book but you will certainly know yourself better. Most of us can face the storm, the typhoon, the sudden thunder. What most of us find difficult is the trough of low pressure, where nothing much happens, in which tomorrow will be the same as yesterday and the barometer needle is sickeningly steady, moving neither up nor down. Ecclesiastes is no gospel but it will help us to recognise the gospel when we hear it.

4 Orthodox and radical
Proverbs and Job

We began our studies in the Old Testament with the book
of Ecclesiastes. I repeat the reasons for so doing: it has a
universal message and it can be understood even at the
distance of more than twenty centuries without any
detailed knowledge of the milieu from which it comes.
Before, however, we move on to the books of Proverbs
and of Job, which are the subject of this chapter, it
would be a help to take a look at that milieu. A casual
acquaintanceship with the Old Testament would suggest
that it is largely composed of bloody battles, shady
intrigues, complicated laws and excruciatingly boring
genealogies. There is, however, another element of which
we are on the whole less aware, which played a dominant
part not only in the literature of the period but in the life
of the people of Israel – and that is the Wisdom tradition.
The prime example of it in the Old Testament is the book
of Proverbs, formally attributed to Solomon as the
fountainhead of all wisdom but in fact varying in authorship
and derived from a variety of sources, not all of them
Hebrew. It is an entrancing book, provided you do not
attempt to read too much of it at once, and it has an air of
modernity. Listen to this, for example, from the first chapter
as it is translated in the Living Bible: 'If young toughs
tell you, "Come and join us" – turn your back on them!
"We'll hide and rob and kill," they say. "Good or bad,
we'll treat them all alike. And the loot we'll get! All
kinds of stuff! Come on, throw in your lot with us, we'll
split with you in equal shares." ' Or listen to this in the
Today's English Version translation from chapter 5
addressing itself to a perennial problem: 'The lips of
another man's wife may be as sweet as honey and her
kisses smooth as olive oil, but when it is all over she
leaves you nothing but bitterness and pain . . . Be faithful
to your wife and give your love to her alone.' Or listen
to this in chapter 26 (same translation) about a problem
which assails us all at some time or another: 'The lazy
man turns over in bed. He's like a door swinging on its
hinges – really going places.' But the Wisdom tradition is
more than a patchwork of apophthegms and proverbs, of

riddles and parables, it is part of a total educational
system common to the ancient world which was designed
to prepare young people for success in government,
agriculture, law, commerce and personal life (see Appendix
4). Israel was part of this ancient world and became even
more so when Jerusalem fell in 587 and the Jewish people
were scattered. The Wisdom literature, therefore, which we
find in the Old Testament, reminds us that Israel did not
and could not live in a ghetto; it was profoundly influenced
by the philosophy, culture and commercial practices of its
particular period. The Bible is not a transcript simply of
Jewish experience but of a universal experience which by
the providence of God, or if you prefer the accidents of
history, has come down to us in Hebrew language, Hebrew
literature and Hebrew categories of thought but is as
relevant to Birmingham as it was to Babylon; is as
significant for a housing estate on Merseyside as for the
suburbs of ancient Rome.

It would be a mistake to attempt to read the book of
Proverbs straight through; like a book of clever sayings
for after-dinner speakers it soon begins to pall. The tone is
sententious or, if you prefer a shorter word, smug, and it
suffers from one grave defect which has been the death of
many such a philosophy ever since. It suggests that the
study and practice of Wisdom will issue in peace, happiness
and success. It could not be better put than at the end of
chapter 11 in the book of Proverbs: 'The righteous shall
be recompensed in the earth'. The book of Ecclesiastes
has already undermined that belief with a kind of sapping
action; the book of Job assaults it with all the artillery at
the author's command. Job is one of the great books of the
world. It is significant that there is just one non-Jewish
heroine within the pages of Scripture – Ruth the Moabitess,
ancestress of David – and one hero, and that is the hero of
the book of Job. He lived in the land of Uz which,
wherever it may be, is not within the confines of Israel. By
this simple literary device the author is inviting us to
attend to a universal problem – the problem of the
suffering of the righteous. As elsewhere in the Bible, the
author takes a familiar story, the story of a righteous man
Job, who endured unmerited suffering (so the old story
went) with exemplary patience. That is not, distinctly
not, the message of the biblical book. Job had many
virtues but patience was not one of them. And it was

precisely because he lacked this gift of patience that he
exposed in such radical form the torments to which
ordinary human beings are subject and the inadequacies
of the smooth things which wise people say about them. In
short, the book of Job is an attack upon the traditional
wisdom of his day. There are many such in our own time,
young men and an occasional middle-aged one, who will
not be consoled by the smooth sayings of their elders;
who will not accept the familiar structures of state and
church and commerce and industry as if they were
sacrosanct; who really want to know what life is about and
why it is as it is. Job was an anarchist in the academic
establishments of his day, not the man you would welcome
as student representative on your university council.

The message of the book is this – it was bad enough to
lose your home and your family and to break out in boils,
and to be put in an isolation ward, but the visitors who
came to sit by your bed day after day made it even worse.
For however polite they may have been, their innermost
conviction, which occasionally breaks out into speech, is
that for all his seeming righteousness Job must have been
a very wicked man. Why otherwise should he suffer so?
Job reacts instinctively. He is no saint, he is aware of that;
nevertheless by the standards of his own day he had been a
good man. Read chapter 31, for example; there is no better
example of the upright life to be found in the literature
of any people. Therefore he cannot, he will not, accept
the verdict of the society in which he lives as represented
by the comforters, and the book is a cry of rage against
the perverters of reason and the pedlars of a utilitarian
morality. That is where, alas, too many of our modern
revolutionaries bow out. They get their cue, they rush on
the stage, they make a fiery speech, they create a commotion
– and then they become stockbrokers. A cry of rage is not
enough – Job is waiting for Godot on his squalid heap
outside the city, in his tattered garments, with his
miserable possessions round him, and only passers-by to
give him cheer.

It follows that the book of Job is not about the problem of
suffering. It is about the relationship between the academic
and the real, between the thoughts men think in their
heads and what they experience in the marrow bone,
between humanism and religion. For indeed the humanists

have no other perspective but the one which the comforters
offer to Job. They desire a happy life, free from pain and
poverty and war, and they prescribe certain means by
which it can be attained. But we all know that pain and
poverty and war are inseparable from life as we know it,
and a dim and distant utopia is no solace for our present
woes. The traditional Wisdom writers, as they are reflected
in the book of Proverbs, were really humanists, and
humanism was as unsatisfying then as it is now. The
author of Job offers no prescription; he insists on
maintaining his integrity and waits for something to
happen – and it does happen. 'Then the Lord answered
Job out of the whirlwind and said . . .' (chapter 38 verse
1). What God said is not all that important, if I may
presume to say so, although the speech is one of the
great pieces of literature of all time; what is significant is
that God speaks at all. There is a sense in which Job is
appealing back from the conventional wisdom of his day
to the more basic theology of the Hebrew people. There
was no explanation for the sufferings of the Hebrew
people in Egypt. God simply spoke and brought them out.
They did not solve their problems in the wilderness; they
had to learn to live with them, sustained by the presence
of God in fire and smoke. They could not be expected to
understand the tragedies and squalors of the Exile, they
simply heard a voice saying, 'Ho, everyone that thirsteth,
come ye to the waters.' If the book of Ecclesiastes is the
thinking man's reaction to prosperity, then the book of
Job is the religious man's reaction to adversity. He waits
for Godot, he has no other resource; he does not seek
answers, he waits for God to act. 'Waiting not seeking we
go our way', said Martin Buber.

There is a striking modernity about the book of Job.
The nearest equivalent to it in contemporary literature is
Kierkegaard's 'Journal', itself a cry of rage against the
traditional philosophy of his day but, more than that, a
painful experience of the reality and presence of God. The
modern man, a few years ago so confident in his technology
and in his limited view of life, now finds himself deprived
of those securities – and there are many comforters in
church and state who are crying 'peace' where there is no
peace. It is the experience of God and that alone which
enables a man to face himself as he really is and to survive
that experience. The story of Job is the story of the

religious man (his religion well hidden most of the time) who because he would not be satisfied with anything less than the truth, found God. The seeming atheist is often a religious man engaged on the same quest. 'I talked about things I did not understand, about marvels too great for me to know. You told me to listen while you spoke and to try to answer your questions. Then I knew only what others had told me, but now I have seen you with my own eyes, so I am ashamed of all I have said and repent in dust and ashes.' (chapter 42)

PROVERBS AND JOB

The book of Proverbs contains eight divisions:
1 In Praise of Wisdom, 1:7 to chap. 9
2 Proverbs of Solomon, 10:1 to 22:16
3 Words of the Wise, 22:17 to 24:22
4 'Sayings of the Wise', 24:23–34
5 'Proverbs of Solomon', 25:1 to 29:27
6 'Words of Agur', 30:1–33
7 'Words of King Lemuel', 31:1–9
8 Praise of a good, efficient wife, 31:10–31.

A brief outline of the book of Job:
1 The Prologue – 1, 2
2 The Poem – 3:1–42:6
  a Job bewails his birth and longs for death – 3
  b Three series of debates –
    (i) Eliphaz, 4, 5; Job, 6, 7; Bildad, 8; Job, 9, 10; Zophar, 11; Job, 12–14.
    (ii) Eliphaz, 15; Job, 16, 17; Bildad, 18; Job, 19; Zophar, 20; Job, 21.
    (iii) Eliphaz, 22; Job, 23, 24; Bildad, 25; Job, 26, 27.
  c The poem on wisdom – 28
  d Job reviews his life – 29–31
  e The speeches of Elihu – 32–37
  f Jehovah speaks – 38–41
  g Job's submission – 42:1–6
3 The Epilogue – 42:7–17.

5

Songs of faith and doubt
The Psalms

My academic friends will lift an eyebrow to see the
Psalms included in what I have called the easier section
of this book. 'Surely', they will say, 'the Psalter provides
us with a range of problems unequalled anywhere else in
the Old Testament', and that is true. Books on the
Psalter written in this century in English alone would
fill a bookshelf or two. 'Moreover', they will say, 'the
Psalter covers such an enormous range of history that it
is important to know something about that history before
one can possibly attempt an interpretation of the Psalms'.
That is true also; the latest of the Psalms may be separated
from the earliest by as much as a thousand years – you
have in your hand a collection of poems, songs, hymns
and folk music as diverse in form and content as a
collected Book of Verse ranging from William the
Conqueror to the present day. They will say that there are
acute linguistic and textual problems that defy the wisdom
of the wise and will not yield to the simplicity of the
simple. All these objections are fair and I shall be alluding
to them in the course of this chapter but I chose to put
the Psalter here for four reasons.

The first is that the Psalms are part of the so-called
Writings, i.e. the third Canon of Scripture, and in Hebrew
tradition at least, therefore, are properly associated with
Ecclesiastes, Proverbs and Job – and indeed they include
in them certain very pronounced Wisdom elements. The
second reason is that almost every reader of this book will
have a passing familiarity with at least one or two of the
Psalms. It is hardly possible to live in England or in the
West generally without, for example, having heard or sung
Psalm 23. It is an indication of the range of emotion
contained in that psalm that it seems to be equally suitable
for weddings and for funerals. The third reason is that
like so much of the Wisdom literature in the third Canon,
the Psalms are capable of being appreciated with the
minimum of technical knowledge, although technical
knowledge does enormously enhance their meaning and
significance. The fourth reason is that they seem to have an

almost universal appeal. I say 'almost universal' because I
am aware, for instance, that certain Arab Christians have
found it extremely difficult to assimilate the Psalter into
their worship, in view of what they regard as the ugly
nationalistic overtones which may be discerned in it. But
it remains true for most of us, who are not trapped within
this particular political dilemma, that we shall find in the
Psalter utterances which exactly express our own needs and
aspirations, whether we are Jews or Greeks, labourers or
laboratory assistants, football fanatics or photographers. Of
the Psalter it may certainly be said that it is a book for all
mankind. Open it at any point and you will find faith –
not just assent but a deep confiding trust in the Lord of
the Universe – and doubt, the honest doubt of one who
faces the complexities of human existence and swings
between the extreme scepticism of the author of
Ecclesiastes and the indefinable awareness of the presence
and power of God as it was revealed to the author of the
book of Job.

But we see in the Psalter a transcript not simply of human
experience, swinging between the two poles of faith and
doubt, but a transcript of the experience of the human
race as that is illustrated in the thousand years of Hebrew
history out of which this book arose. There is a sense in
which you will learn far more about the Victorian era from
prose, the plays and the poetry of the good Queen's day
than you will ever learn from the solemn procession of
events which our forefathers were pleased to call 'history'.
You would expect, therefore, to find the salient features of
Israel's history reflected in the Psalms. David himself was
known as 'the sweet singer of Israel' and there need be no
serious doubt that there are psalms from his own hand.
Some of the psalms too may well allude to precise historical
circumstances, though without any certainty that they
actually do so. You would expect to find echoes of the
battles, the victories, the defeats of a nation almost
constantly at war with its neighbours. You will find
psalms from the dispersion as well as from within
Palestine, e.g. 'By the waters of Babylon we sat down and
wept' (Ps. 137). And almost everywhere in the Psalter
you will trace the influence of the prophets. Some of them
were writers and singers themselves (for example, the
'Song of the Vineyard' by Isaiah in chapter 5). But the
prophets' literary influence on the Psalms is as nothing

compared with their enormous spiritual influence – their insistence upon spiritual reality, their demand that the people should trust and not just believe, their call to repentance and renewal, their vision of a new world where men live in love and peace with one another and God is over all. 'When God is over all' – that is perhaps the supreme message of the Psalter; grave and gay, these writers, poets and thinkers ultimately rest on this strange assurance, so typical of their people as a whole, that the Lord is King. If that is true at all, it must be true for all. If the people of Israel were right, they hold in trust a precious revelation which is for the salvation of all mankind – the Lord is King.

My academic friends are right; there are certain problems associated with the Psalms which are not immediately obvious to the man revelling in the beautiful cadences of the Prayer Book version or to the boy singing lustily in the village choir. For the more serious student, however, an examination of these problems could give a resonance and depth to his understanding of the Psalter and it is to these problems that I now turn.

The study of the Psalter in universities and theological colleges this century has been dominated by the attempt to provide some workable classification. The Bible itself provides a classification of a kind: there are the Psalms of David (largely books 1 and 2); there are the Psalms of Asaph (a guild of musicians); the Psalms of the sons of Korah (a guild of singers); there are the Songs of Ascents (Psalms 120–134) believed to have been sung by pilgrims on their way to Jerusalem; there are two groups of Hallelujah Psalms (111–118 and 146–150) marked by the same opening sentence, 'Praise the Lord'. Some versions of the Bible have tried to improve on this classification by suggesting historical contexts from which a particular psalm may have arisen. In our century, however, study has centred on an attempt to classify according to the form which the psalm takes, or the locality around which a group of psalms may have gathered, or the use to which the psalms may have been put in public worship. I hope I shall not sound disparaging if I simply say that this has been a useful exercise but the results of it are far from assured. May I take one simple example to illustrate the difficulties of even the most elementary classification. In book 2 and

the first half of book 3, the name for God is '*Elohim*'; in
the rest of the Psalter, with one or two exceptions, the
normal name is 'The Lord' ('*Yahweh*'). This is, of course, a
familiar feature in the Pentateuch, to which we shall be
returning later, but what are we to make of it in the
Psalms? Does it suggest that one group of psalms grew
up in a different locality? or around a different shrine? or
reflected a different theological standpoint? Dan is after
all a long way from Beer-sheba and there must have been
substantial variations of religious custom and belief
amongst the tribes.

I turn now to a more far-reaching issue. It is only too
easy for us who live in the West and whose knowledge
of an oriental literature is confined to the Bible, to assume
that the Hebrew people lived in a kind of enclave, reared
their children, made their bargains, built their houses and
harvested their crops in a ghetto. This has, of course, been
true of some tribes in the history of the world – the
Eskimo separated from his fellow human beings within
his Arctic wastes; the Pygmy trapped in his jungle lacking
any communication with the outside world over a period
of centuries. This is not true of Israel. Apart from a
relatively short period in what the Bible calls 'the
wilderness' they lived out their lives at the heart of the
great imperial structures of the ancient world – in
Mesopotamia, in Egypt, in Canaan, in the Roman Empire
(see Appendix 4). They are a peculiar people no doubt,
but they do not walk alone, and the Bible everywhere
shows evidences of cross-fertilisation, between what we
have come to call the distinctive religion of the Hebrews
and the other religions of the ancient world. In Northern
Syria in 1928 a farmer's plough exposed an ancient tomb
and the full-scale excavations which followed exposed the
ancient city of Ugarit (now Ras Shamra). The discoveries
made there have thrown a flood of light upon that
civilisation which Israel entered when they crossed the
Jordan into the Promised Land. The pages of the book of
Joshua are full of the battles which the Israelites fought
to establish themselves over against the earlier inhabitants
of Canaan. What is not so well documented is that inner
struggle with the religious and cultural forces they found
there. In this field it was not a question of victory or
defeat but rather of 'appropriation and transformation'.
That was precisely the title given by Professor Harvey

Guthrie of Cambridge, Massachusetts, to a series of lectures
upon the Psalter which he gave at St. George's College,
Jerusalem, in 1974. The Psalter is the product of this
steady process of 'appropriation and transformation', in
which the religion of the wilderness appropriates and
transforms the religion of the farm and the city.

Take an example from a different period of Israel's history –
Psalm 91. The man revelling in the cadences of the Prayer
Book version or the boy singing lustily in the choir could
not be expected to know that this particular psalm is
thought to be full of allusions to demons and magic and
witches, elements which would seem to be entirely absent
from the earlier traditions of Israel – once again an example
of 'appropriation and transformation'. I make this point
with some care because I wish you to see that in the Bible
we are not dealing with a series of documents which
dropped down from heaven ready-made in order that we
might incorporate them into our liturgy. They arose out
of the struggle in the hearts and minds of a peculiar
people who had their faith tested and developed in a
cultural situation not as dissimilar to our own as we might
think, where affluence was the measure of success, where
profit was the index of progress and where true religion
had a hard struggle to survive. The Bible does not arise
out of the religion of Israel alone. It arises out of that
religion as it was influenced by and as it reacted to the
religion of those amongst whom the Hebrews lived – in
Egypt, in Canaan, in Babylon, in Greece. We are the
beneficiaries of a long process of 'appropriation and
transformation'.

Before we launch out on to the next main section of the
Bible, it would be an appropriate moment to say something
about methods of reading it. It needs to be read with
discrimination, approaching it as you would approach
any library of books. Some books can only be read straight
through if they are to make any sense, and that would
certainly apply to books like Ecclesiastes and Job, Genesis
and Jonah. No one would think of reading Dickens or
Sartre half a page at a time. There are other books, however,
which require the more reflective approach and the
Psalter is certainly in this category. Nobody would read
Hymns Ancient and Modern from cover to cover and expect
to derive much benefit from it. The Psalms therefore have

to be read as the writers wrote them – reflectively, allowing
the message to rest on the mind, listening across the
centuries to the voice of God as he made himself known in
the mind of this Jewish merchant in Tyre or this Hebrew
farmer in Tekoa or this woman drawing water from the
well at Beer-sheba or this boy serving at the altar in
Shiloh. You may never be able to make the pilgrimage to
these places but you need to make this pilgrimage in heart
and mind every time you read the Psalms. They are written
by real people out of a real experience in a real world.

PSALMS: THE HYMNBOOK OF HUMANITY

Five books: 1–41
              42–72
              73–89
              90–106
              107–150

This division was an imitation of the 5 books of the
Pentateuch.

The Psalms which spoke to the early Church as having
been fulfilled in Jesus Christ were: 2, 8, 16, 22, 31, 40, 68,
69, 89, 102, 110, 118.

6 A change of key
From Writings to Prophecy

I never cease to wonder at the skill and artistry with which
the professional musician moves from one key to another.
We now have to attempt a literary modulation from the
'Writings' of the Hebrew Canon to the histories. But first
of all a word about the section we are now leaving. The
'Writings' include the books which we have already
studied (Ecclesiastes, Proverbs, Job and Psalms) and the
only other substantial part of the 'Writings' is the work of
the Chronicler (1/2 Chronicles and Ezra–Nehemiah).
These books would, however, be inexplicable without
some reference to the history of Israel and we shall,
therefore, have to return to them later.

The Psalms speak a universal language, echoing the
universal experience of mankind – frustration, suffering,
aspiration; they can be understood by anyone, anywhere,
with the minimum of technical knowledge, and they are
each the product of an individual mind. It is true, of course,
that they passed through various stages of development
and were no doubt modified by subsequent editors but
with one or two exceptions they began as the product of a
particular person, in a particular place, wrestling with
moods of doubt and faith, despair and hope. There were
no doubt many thousands of such songs current in Israel
at various stages in its life. It was the literary excellence
and the spiritual insight which ensured for a mere one
hundred and fifty of these psalms and songs a permanent
place in the documents of Israel and in the liturgy of the
Temple. 'Abide with me' began as an individual's spiritual
experience before it became part of a football Cup Final
ritual. 'Rock of Ages' was the heartfelt utterance of a
man in need of salvation before it became one of the
hymns for Good Friday.

The modulation from this particular key to the next is
not an easy one to achieve. We move from the exalted
sentiments of the Psalms to the rather tiresome details of
Israel's history. We move from the universal to the
sectarian, from the immediately relevant to the seemingly

irrelevant. Yet we shall have to observe that the Hebrew
people themselves attached comparatively little significance
to the 'Writings' (the third Canon) and much more
significance to the second Canon and to the historical
writings which comprise part of it.

Here we need to pause and observe that the second Canon
is called 'The Prophets'. The long books from Joshua to the
end of 2 Kings are the 'Former Prophets' and what we are
accustomed to call 'The Prophets' they called the 'Latter
Prophets' (see Appendix 2). It will make our reading of
the histories more bearable if we take the Hebrew title
seriously. Those who are not professional historians tend
to think that history is an exact science, that all you have
to do is to gather the relevant documents, put them in the
right order and you have written a history. If you are one
of those who still nurture this illusion, you will find the
Bible itself a powerful dissuasive. Read, for example, the
accounts of the same series of events as they are presented
to us on the one hand by the book of Kings and on the
other by the Chronicles – the same series of events, the
same 'facts', but an entirely different impression. That could
be one of the reasons why the Hebrews called the history of
their people 'prophecy' – because it was the function of a
prophet to discern the times and to draw conclusions from
them. Those who took the trouble (and it was a lot of
trouble) to write Joshua, Judges, 1/2 Samuel and 1/2
Kings, did so not for their own amusement or profit, nor
to get good reviews in the newspaper, but to say
something not only about the past but about the future,
not only about what had happened but what those
happenings meant. There is no such thing as plain,
unbiased history. The business of giving shape and
meaning, an air of verisimilitude to an otherwise bald and
unconvincing narrative, is an art as well as a science, and
the historian is a valued member of any thinking
community ancient or modern. When, therefore, you
face the formidable task of reading the history of Israel
in the 'Former Prophets', I hope, like the prophets
themselves, you will learn to read between the lines, to ask
the questions – what is the author trying to say and why is
he saying it? Any history-book worthy of the name will
tell you at least as much about the person who wrote it as
about the people he is writing about.
We seek, therefore, to enter into the mind of, say, an

author living in the fifth or fourth century BC, after the Exile, as he reflects on the centuries of Hebrew history which preceded him. Whether he be a member of the establishment in Jerusalem or of the intelligentsia in Alexandria, or of a monastic community, such an approach will make the battles, the intrigues, the treaties, the tragedies of Israel's history not simply bearable but fruitful in our understanding of the history of all mankind. When we see history through the eyes of the biblical interpreter, we have a glimpse into all history; we acquire a philosophy of history, we become students of and not simply dabblers in history; we learn to take history seriously as an illustration of the hand of God at work in human affairs.

When we move from the 'Writings' to the 'Prophets', from the heartfelt sentiments of the Psalms to the painstaking efforts of the Hebrew historian, we move into another key. But the theme remains – the Lord is King.

7 Political theology
Joshua, Judges, Samuel, Kings

Political theology is the kind of theology we have come to
associate with the Christian–Marxist dialogue or the
liberation movements or the development issue in the third
world. But there is nothing new under the sun and there
is a whole section of the Old Testament which can only
be styled political theology. It is to be found in the second
'canon' of scripture (see Appendix 2) which comprises the
former Prophets (Joshua, Judges, Samuel, Kings) and the
latter Prophets (the 'big three', then Hosea to Malachi).
This whole section is concerned with politics – not party
politics which has no counterpart in the ancient world –
but politics just the same – that is, how people live
together in communities, how authority is exercised and
under what restraints. Once the patriarchal or nomadic
style of life is left behind, politics inevitably supervenes.
When the people of Israel entered Canaan and settled
there they became not just a religious or a tribal unit but
a political unit. The books Joshua, Judges, Samuel and
Kings trace the process by which the Hebrews achieved
their own characteristic political structures and how they
fared under them. But that history was more than a bare
recital of events. The authors, as we shall see later, were
themselves under the influence of five centuries of
prophecy and in their hands the history became the
vehicle for a message which far transcended any of the
political structures under which Israel happened to be
living at any particular time. Politics thus gave rise to a
theology – that is, 'political theology'. It is to this that
we now turn and trace the development of a theology which
took shape around the person of David.

Any visitor to the performance of the 'Son et Lumiere' at
the Citadel in Jerusalem will be exposed to a cold wind
even after the hottest summer day, and he will be exposed
to something else as well – to the fervid adulation of King
David. Perhaps that is not so surprising after all because
the action is taking place in the City of David and the
present Israelis certainly feel the need for the warlike
qualities and the diplomatic finesse which were so

characteristic of their great ancestor. But it may be
surprising to us, nevertheless, because we have been
reared on the documents of the Hebrew people rather than
on a knowledge of their actual life and traditions, and we
tend, therefore, to dwell on what we might call the
spiritual giants of the Old Testament for our inspirational
reading, e.g. Abraham, Moses, Elijah, Isaiah, etc. David
is by any standards a great man wondrously devoted to his
Lord and a singularly attractive person, but he is not to be
compared with the spiritual giants of the race. Nevertheless
he commands a larger space than any of them in the Old
Testament and if you live in an age where writing material
is in short supply and writing is laborious, that is always
a fair indication of the importance attached to a particular
subject or to a particular person. Does David merit the
space which is devoted to him? Historically, No. The
truth is that the city which David captured in a most
spectacular way bore little resemblance to the city of more
recent antiquity and did in fact lie outside the present
City walls. It was little more than a village on a hill. The
so-called empire over which David reigned was for the
greater part of his time a territory not much larger than
Wales. The fragile unity which he achieved between the
tribes did not long outlast his death and the prestige which
Israel acquired as the result of his success, impressive
though it was to those who lived in the narrow enclave of
Syria and Palestine, must have seemed of little account to
those familiar with the majestic empires of Egypt and
Babylon (Appendix 4). Are we to say then, that the author
of 1/2 Samuel was simply a dissimulator, one who looked
back across the centuries through a hazy glow?

This is the point at which we shall have to take seriously
something to which I referred in the previous chapter,
namely, the experience and background of the author
himself. However many minds contributed to the
writing of Israel's history (and they would be many)
someone at some point took the whole matter in hand and
'published' what we now know as 1 and 2 Samuel and
1 and 2 Kings. That person must have done his work after
the last event described in the book and that event is the
destruction of Israel and the demise of the Davidic
monarchy. Is he then compensating for the tragedies of
the present by magnifying the achievements of the past?
Is he, like the author of Daniel, looking out of his

windows in Babylon towards Jerusalem, nostalgic for the Davidic monarchy at the highest point of its power? He might well be forgiven for doing so; the present was insupportable, the future grim and only the past had any glory in it. But we must remember that the writer was not an annalist simply but a theologian or, to put it another way, a prophet.

The beginning of the reign of David can be dated with reasonable certainty at 1000 BC. It is, however, more than a fixed point in history, it is a fixed point in the theology of Israel around which the life and imagination of that people revolved. His reign may have been only partially successful, his conquests temporary, his capital city little more than a village on the hill, but he assumed stupendous importance in the theology of Israel and subsequently in the theology of the Christian Church. Jesus of Nazareth was called 'the Son of David'. To understand this phenomenon, we shall have to go back in history to the events which led up to the foundation of the Hebrew monarchy.

Huge uncertainties attach to the process by which the people of Israel established themselves in the Promised Land but I think it can now be said with reasonable confidence that two or three hundred years before the reign of David a group of Semitic people, known in the contemporary records as the Habiru, swept across the Jordan and caused extreme alarm and confusion amongst the peoples of the land (see Appendix 4). At best the people of Israel at that stage constituted a loose confederacy of tribes; at their worst they fell out with each other and sometimes held aloof from the conflicts in which their fellow tribesmen were involved. The conquest of Canaan was haphazard and piecemeal, with the Israelites strong in some places and weak in others, always threatened by those recent settlers called 'Philistines' along the coastal strip, and fiercely resisted by some of the original inhabitants of the land. Joshua was a leader of some renown, but no great leader succeeded to him; hence the steady lament which runs like a threnody through the book of Judges – 'there was no king in Israel; everyone did that which was right in his own eyes'. The political dream of the nineteenth century AD was the political nightmare of the twelfth century BC. At a crucial moment

Samuel, a prophet like Moses, arose, a powerful though
shadowy figure, whose influence on the subsequent
history of the Hebrews and of the Christian Church was
profound and far-reaching. Whilst he lived he imposed his
spiritual authority on the people as a whole but as the
author of 1 Samuel sadly records, his sons did not follow
in his steps. So it was that a popular movement arose in
Israel, when Samuel grew older, agitating for the
appointment of a king on a par with the kings of the
other nations. At this point in the narrative confusion
creeps in and the normal explanation is that there are two
accounts of the establishment of the monarchy, which the
post-exilic editor allowed to stand side by side without
attempting to harmonise them (1 Samuel ch. 8, also 10:
17–25; and 1 Samuel 9:1–10:16). This particular
phenomenon you will have to get used to in the Bible. It
occurs again, for example, in the early chapters of the book
of Genesis and in the Synoptic accounts of our Lord's
life. We need not attempt a harmonisation of the Synoptic
Gospels, nor of the two accounts of the origin of the
Hebrew monarchy. Let the authors speak for themselves.
They stand for two theological attitudes towards the
monarchy, both of which were present not only in the
mind of the editor of 1/2 Samuel but in the mind of the
people as a whole. The two attitudes may be roughly
described as follows.

The first is that the monarchy was a disaster from the
beginning; that the people of Israel ought to have been
satisfied with the kind of charismatic leadership which was
available to them in Moses, in the Judges, in Samuel and in
the prophets; that the monarchy was directly or indirectly
responsible for most of the abuses which disfigured national
life and produced the hunger for territorial expansion, for
luxury, for military success, for worldly values which the
pious observer of Hebrew life could only regret. The demise
of the monarchy, therefore, in 587 was only to be expected;
the fall of Jerusalem and the death of the King was God's
judgement upon a decision forced upon Samuel by the
people some five centuries before. Indeed the fall of
Jerusalem was to be welcomed and the death of the
monarch accepted as the means by which, in God's
providence, the people of Israel were to be restored to
their proper role as God's special people, special in their
laws, special in their form of government, special in their

attitude to the world, special in their abhorrence of secular nationalism. The issue is far from dead; this is precisely the attitude which some orthodox Jews take towards the modern State of Israel. In their view the modern State of Israel has forfeited the right to exist because it has blatantly accepted worldly values which are at variance with the true purpose of Israel. Military adventures, international treaties, social engineering, political manoeuvres, are all alike abhorrent to them. The true Israel is the servant people of God, content if necessary to live in its ghetto, to preserve and study the Torah and to magnify their differences from the nations around them. To them the ultimate blasphemy is to wish to be like the other nations. This attitude is reflected in one of the accounts (1 Samuel ch. 8), where Samuel is shown as accepting the people's initiative with bad grace and predicting all the disasters which in his view would follow from it. 'How right Samuel was', these orthodox would say.

The other account (1 Samuel ch. 9) presents a different picture. It is of a process which took place under the hand of God and by his providence, and this is made clear by the extraordinary circumstances under which Saul was introduced to Samuel and, at the drop of a hat, was anointed King of Israel. He was just another young man, who might have remained a farmer like his father had he not gone out looking for his father's lost asses. Having despaired of finding them by their own efforts, he and his servant sought the advice of the local prophet, who could be expected to tell the future or to uncover the past on payment of a fee. The prophet, however, proved to be none other than the great Samuel himself who happened to be there for the festival. Samuel had already been prepared by God for the encounter; he took the encounter to be the sign of God's choice of Saul as king and after the minimum of preparation anointed him as such.

Before we consider the implications of this second account may I say in passing how important it is to allow for the element of humour in the Old Testament. It is very marked in this particular passage – the comic circumstances (looking for lost asses), the future King of Israel without a penny in his pocket, the embarrassment of mistaking the great Samuel himself for a fortune teller. It is a pity that the Bible is read in churches with such unvarying solemnity so alien to the sharp allusive humour of the original authors. The humour aside – what are the implications of this second account? It suggests a qualified approval of the monarchy, seeing it as the consequence of the direct will of God made explicit in the providential encounter between Samuel and Saul. What was wrong with it in practice was that the kings of Israel sought to be like the other kings of the ancient world, invoking arbitrary rights, overturning the liberties of the subjects, undermining the fabric of traditional Hebrew life. I ask you to observe that somewhat mysterious verse (1 Samuel 10:25) about 'the manner of the kingdom', which presumably related to a body of law governing the relationship between the king and his people and setting limits to his power. The fact is that the kings of Israel were no worse and often much better than the kings of the other nations. They were to a greater extent than was common in the ancient world constitutional monarchs, controlled by a system of law which stood over against them. They were conscious of their social responsibilities even although they neglected them. They listened to the prophets even though they did not always obey them. But like every other king they were trapped in the problem of authority. Who was to exercise it? To whom was he responsible? Under what restraints and with what limitations was he entitled to exercise power? (1 Kings ch. 21) The problem still troubles the Church as it troubles the nation. It troubles the Town Council and the University. Political theology is an attempt to grapple with it.

Any historian, as we have seen, is bound to rely upon his sources and those sources may well reflect varying theological opinion. Thus two opinions of the founding of the monarchy and the implications of it are to be found within the pages of 1 Samuel. In the end, however, at some point in time some person had to make himself responsible for the ultimate shape of the whole book. Are we entitled to draw any conclusions from the book as a whole as it relates to the vexed problem of authority? One thing is certainly clear, that is, that the author did not prescribe any alternative forms of government or give his accolade to one rather than the other. The Hebrew people were to suffer under many forms of authority – theocratic (the High Priest), bureaucratic (the Sanhedrin), imperialist (Roman) and revolutionary (the Maccabees). It does not

appear that the Hebrews as a whole were any better off
under one system than another. Must we conclude,
therefore, that there is no such thing as a political
theology? Shall we have to collapse into the ultimate
scepticism – 'What's the point of an election? It means
putting one lot of sinners out and putting another lot of
sinners in'? Such a saying might well have been
attributed to the author of the book Ecclesiastes in line
with his general scepticism about life, but not so in the
greater part of the Hebrew tradition where politics and
theology were inseparable – prophets constantly meddled
in politics. If the author did not prescribe any alternative
method of government, is there anything else which we
may deduce from the form which the book ultimately
took? Only this – the author clearly observed in the reign
of David something infinitely suggestive for the principle
of authority as a whole. For David was a man after God's
own heart, ruling in the fear of the Lord. It could be said
of him, as it could seldom be said of any of his successors,
that for the greater part of his reign he sought to live in
obedience to the God who had called him. He recognised
that such authority as he possessed was an authority
derived from God alone. It is a rather striking fact that the
prophets, when they sought to descry the outlines of the
future society, seemed to look not only forward, but
backward to the reign of David, the man after God's
own heart, the ideal King, the one who ruled as the vice-
regent of God.

I have studiously resisted the temptation so far to look to
the New Testament as an explanation of the Old, because
there is a sense in which the Old Testament stands in its
own right. Jesus of Nazareth and his followers had no
other scriptures. To them it was the revelation of God
once delivered by the hand of Moses and the voice of the
prophets. But Jesus of Nazareth was and was known as
'the Son of David'. The assumptions that his countrymen
made about David found their focus, so his immediate
followers believed, in the person of Jesus. It was even
believed by many of them that he was there and then to
reconstitute the kingdom and to reign over it as David
his ancestor had done. There is a connection between
David and David's greater son and that connection is
exemplified in Jesus's unfailing obedience to his father's
will. He was a King indeed but one who acknowledged

the supreme Kingship of God and expressed his monarchy
in terms of service. It was a representative of the hated
Roman Empire who saw it more clearly than most when
he observed, 'You are a man under authority'. Like the
historian we have been studying in this chapter, our Lord
did not prescribe the form of the new society, the exact
nature of 'the Kingdom' which dominated his mind. He
merely reiterated the great truth everywhere present in the
Old Testament that it is the Lord who is King and that
any subordinate authority, indispensable though it is to
government, can only operate effectively when it is 'under
authority' – the authority of God himself. This is the
message of the Former Prophets but it only became
capable of articulation when a greater than David appeared
on the human scene. It has far-reaching implications for
governments and nations, for reactionaries and
revolutionaries alike.

SUGGESTED READINGS

Joshua 3:1–17
Judges 5:1–31
1 Samuel 9:1–17
1 Samuel 17:21–50
2 Samuel 12:1–25

1 Kings 10:1–13
1 Kings 18:20–46
2 Kings 5:1–19
2 Kings 23:1–25

8 Let the Church be the Church
Deuteronomy

It may seem odd to interpose at this point between a
chapter on the Former Prophets and a chapter on the
Latter Prophets, a chapter on Deuteronomy. The reader is
entitled to know the reasons – and here they are.

The first is a simple one – that there is a section in it
which alludes to the establishment of the monarchy and
comments on it (17:14–20). The second reason, which is
slightly more complicated, is that the book is confidently
claimed to be the 'book of the law' which was discovered
in the Temple in the reign of Josiah and revolutionised
the life of that king and of his kingdom (2 Kings chs.
22, 23). Of him alone, of the kings of Israel after David,
the author was able to say, 'No king before him had
turned to the Lord as he did, with all his heart and soul
and strength, following the law of Moses, nor did any king
like him appear again' (2 Kings 23:25). The third reason
is that the book occupies an important place in the
development of Hebrew literature and it is scarcely possible
to proceed further with our studies without taking it into
account (see Appendix 3). So now to a long digression on
the publishing business in ancient Israel.

There are certain important questions which you should
address to any book of the Bible as you begin to read it.
The first is, 'What sort of book is this?' In some cases
this is easy enough to answer. It should be obvious to the
most casual reader, provided the translators have done
their job, whether it is prose or poetry. Ecclesiastes is
prose; Job is poetry. But it is not always as easy as that.
What about, for example, the book of Jonah? Is that
narrative, or prophecy or satire? Or the book of Genesis,
is it theology or mythology? If you take the gossip
column from 'The Sun' and wrongly imagine it to be a
leading article in 'The Times', you may well get the
wrong message!

The second question is, 'When was it written?' In a
modern book that is easily answered, for the date is

invariably on, or very near, the title-page. In the Bible this
is not so easy. There are very few positive dates to be had
and in any case there may be some considerable disparity
between the date of a particular section within a book and
the completion date for the whole book. Some sections of
the Pentateuch, for example, may well date from before
the monarchy and it is possible that others come from
after the Exile. Still, even an elementary commentary will
give you a few dates to choose from and the act of
choosing may well be instructive in itself.

The third question is, 'Who wrote it?' There was no
reward for authorship in the ancient world and no money
to be made out of it. There are only one or two places in
the Old Testament where we may be confident about the
name of the person writing, e.g. the memoirs of Ezra
and Nehemiah, or the writings of Baruch the scribe in
Jeremiah. But it is not impossible, even where the name is
not known, to arrive at an estimate of what kind of person
wrote the book. So one could get answers like this – an
annalist at the court of King David; a priest at one of the
local shrines; a pedagogue in Jerusalem; a Jewish scribe
exiled in Babylon; a poet of the Greek period. It would be
a useful exercise, after you have read a book of the Old
Testament, to write at the beginning of it what sort of
person you think wrote it – old, young, sophisticated,
simple, believer, sceptic, romantic, realist, priest or
prophet.

The fourth question is, 'With what intention did he
write?' A modern author, unless he is of the 'impressionist'
type, leaves you in no doubt as to his intention. He spells
it out in preface and introduction and epilogue. The
ancient author, however, expected you to deduce it from
the content of his book or from the little glimpses he may
give you within the book itself. It is by no means always as
obvious as in the case of the fourth Gospel – 'this is
written that you might believe' (John 20:31) – though
sometimes, as in the book of Jonah, the author can give
you a very broad hint by using words and images which
would have made his intention perfectly clear to those
already familiar with those words and images. That is
just the problem; we are not familiar with them. We tend
to read the Bible in a vacuum, divorced from the everyday
life of its authors and disconcertingly innocent of the kind

of historical and cultural background which, if we are reading a twentieth-century book, we take for granted.

There is one more question which probably would not even occur to most casual readers of the Old Testament and it is this: 'By what means and under what conditions did this book which I am reading achieve public circulation, and then find a place in a collection of writings and ultimately be accepted as part of Sacred Scripture?' There may be excellent books which answer this question satisfactorily but I have yet to find one and I shall, therefore, have to spend a little time addressing myself to these points. I have no reason to believe that I can answer the question any better than my predecessors, but I think that any reader of the Bible must at least be aware of the problem and, if possible, allow his imagination to be kindled by attempting to answer it for himself. The process in the modern world is simple and we know it well. A man may write a book either because he has something he wishes to say or because he is short of money or because he has been commissioned by publishers to do so. He produces the script and from that moment the publisher takes over. The book is printed, reviewed and circulated. A copy of even the most ephemeral book in English is given to the Bodleian Library in Oxford and to the British Museum. It may form part of a series written by the author himself or part of a series written by a collection of authors. It may become a text book and be widely distributed in the schools. If it proves to be a work of genius or becomes the standard authority on a particular subject, it may be maintained in some kind of circulation not simply for decades but for centuries, acquire prestige, be bound in calf, and occupy a prominent position in the library.

Now can we transpose this process and make any sense of it in the ancient world? We ought to be disabused of any notion that the inhabitants of Babylon or Alexandria or Egypt or, for that matter, Jerusalem, were barbarians. On the contrary they were the inheritors of a sophisticated literary tradition (see Appendix 4) and some of the libraries, e.g. Alexandria and Caesarea, enjoyed international repute. The literature which we have in the Bible is one with the literature of the ancient world. The only difference is that it happens, because of its religious

associations with a great institution (Judaism), to have
been preserved, and to have achieved an enormous
currency in the world over a large area and over a very
long period, until it presents itself to us now in black
bindings and gilt lettering, under the title 'Holy Bible'.

There are certain obvious centres around which literary
collections would have been made. Every oriental court
had its annalist, and David's court was no exception; every
shrine had its own little library of holy books; every choir
had its repertoire of sacred music. In such ways we can
account for the preservation and transmission of quite
large sections of the Old Testament (the Psalms, Chronicles,
Ezra-Nehemiah, the Pentateuch).

There is one main section, however, which is not so easily
accommodated, and that is the series of writings which we
have just studied (Joshua, Judges, Samuel, Kings) and the
writings we are about to study (the Prophets). It is not too
difficult to account for the latter. We know that there were
schools or bands of prophets in ancient Israel (see 1
Samuel 10:5; 2 Kings 2:3; 2 Kings 9:1). It was presumably
in these schools that the sayings of the prophets, together
with certain biographical details about them, were
recorded, recited, collected and subsequently transmitted to
posterity. But what about the first group (Joshua, Judges,
Samuel and Kings)? Where did they originate? Under
what conditions were they collected and preserved? What
person or group of persons was responsible for them?

This is where after so long a digression we return to
Deuteronomy. You may be surprised to learn that there
are scholars who would say that Deuteronomy properly
belongs to the second Canon rather than to the first, i.e.
to the Prophets rather than to the Pentateuch. Stylistically
and theologically, so the argument goes, Deuteronomy is
all of a piece with Joshua, Judges, Samuel and Kings. If
this is so, then the writer is one who has been much
influenced by the prophetic tradition and is writing more
an introduction to prophecy than an epilogue to Moses.
The attribution to Moses is, after all, a familiar literary
convention which the author does little to sustain. Instead
he is out to prove the point that has been made time after
time by the prophets that the preservation of Israel depends
utterly on their adherence to the law of God as revealed

to Moses. This is the message of the prophets as a whole. It could be, therefore, that Joshua, Judges, Samuel and Kings (and possibly Deuteronomy) were preserved, like the sayings of the prophets, in the prophetic schools, thus providing a kind of historical background to the sayings and communicating the same message, though in a different literary form. And the message is this – 'Let the Church be the Church': not just the temple building to which the people were inordinately attached, not just the home of the sacrificial ritual upon which they relied, not just a nation like other nations – but the people of God, loyal to God's law and committed to God's purpose in the world.

May I suggest that you begin your studies in the book Deuteronomy by reading the whole of chapter 4 – one of the great literary masterpieces of the Old Testament and the best statement on record of the origins and purpose of the Church – and then compare it with your own Church, your own congregation, your own meeting house or the chapel as you experience it down the road. If you find yourself unduly critical of institutions, then turn to Deuteronomy 6, verse 5 and hear the word of command to the individual which Jesus subsequently made his own – 'You are to love the Lord your God with all your heart, with all your soul, and with all your might, and these words which I command you this day shall be upon your heart and you shall teach them diligently unto your children and you shall talk of them when you are sitting in your house and when you are walking in the street and when you lie down and when you rise up.' No book of the Bible summons the Church more urgently to be the Church.

DEUTERONOMY

See above. Begin with ch. 4.
Jesus and the New Testament writers used Deuteronomy frequently:

Jesus	N.T. Writers
Matthew 4:4 –	Acts 3:22 –
Deuteronomy 8:3	Deuteronomy 18:15, 18
Matthew 4:7 –	1 Corinthians 9:9 –
Deuteronomy 6:16	Deuteronomy 25:4

Matthew 4:10 –
  Deuteronomy 6:13
Matthew 5:31 –
  Deuteronomy 24:1
Mark 12:30 –
  Deuteronomy 6:4–5

2 Corinthians 13:1 –
  Deuteronomy 19:15
Galatians 3:13 –
  Deuteronomy 21:23
Romans 10:6–8 –
  Deuteronomy 30:12, 14

9 The real revolutionaries
From Amos to Malachi

'Don't shoot the pianist, he is doing his best.' Anyone
who attempts an introduction to the Prophets of Israel
within the compass of a single chapter is entitled to ask
for your mercy. If we are content with the so-called
Messianic passages read at Christmas in our churches or
the purple passages which we sometimes read on great
occasions in Church and State, so be it. We shall
undoubtedly profit from them as from any word of the
Lord but once we set about the serious reading of the
Prophets then difficulties abound. They could be summed
up under four headings.

1. The state of the text;
2. The historical background;
3. The origins of prophecy;
4. The unity of the message.

Difficulties about the text arise in two distinct ways. The
first is the text itself upon which our translations have to
be based. If, for example, you are using the Revised
Standard Version of Hosea you will observe at the foot of
every page a large number of alternative readings. The
fact of the matter is that the text of the book of the
prophet Hosea is in places almost impenetrable and it is
doubtful whether we are ever going to be able to improve
on it in any significant way. This must not discourage you
from reading this warm, compassionate book but you
will have to be patient with its obscurities. As an example
of the other kind of difficulty, I refer you to the book of
the prophet Isaiah. It is now widely recognised that it is
composed of three main sections – chapters 1–39 dating
in the main from before the Exile, chapters 40–55 from after
the Exile, chapters 56 to the end, of late but indeterminate
period. But even within the sections, notably within the
first section, the oracles, as they are called, are not in any
obvious order. It is a matter of conjecture, therefore,
whether a particular oracle comes from an early part of the
prophet's life or a later part of it, whether it applies to this
historical circumstance or to another, whether it is the work
of the prophet himself or of a disciple writing in his name.

If, therefore, you propose to yourself a serious study of the
Prophets you are going to need the kind of help that only
a commentary can provide, or at least an introduction like
J. B. Phillips' *Four Prophets* (see Appendix 1).

The second difficulty is a historical one. The prophetic
era is virtually co-extensive with the Hebrew monarchy
(see Appendix 3). That is to say, it covers a period of some
500 years and it is not always obvious at what particular
point in that history the prophets fit in. We do not always
understand why they speak at a particular point or to
what situation they are speaking. They seem to respond
to some cue known only to themselves, march on to the
stage of history, speak their lines and then disappear
again into the obscurity from which they came. They
strut and shout and posture, address themselves to unseen
adversaries, leaving us with the impression that they are
queer, uncomfortable, inexplicable people – actors in a
drama we do not entirely comprehend. They seem, like
the King of Salem, to be without father, without mother,
without genealogy, having neither beginning of days nor
end of life. So we must try to understand something of
their background and the kind of cue to which they
respond so painfully and sometimes so violently. This
brings us to the third difficulty regarding the origins of
prophecy.

I have suggested in a previous chapter that the prophetic
writings as a whole, both Former and Latter, may well
have been preserved, copied and transmitted in the
so-called prophetic schools of which we have tantalisingly
brief glimpses within the Sacred Scriptures themselves.
What were these prophetic schools, why did they come into
existence and what happened in them? Prophecy is not an
isolated phenomenon associated exclusively with the
Hebrew people. In the period we are considering prophets
played a not inconsiderable part in the life of the court,
in the life of the sanctuary and in the life of the nation.
Balaam, that mysterious figure, was not a Hebrew prophet
but was reckoned by the author of Numbers to be in
receipt of the word of God and to be a genuine oracle-
maker (Numbers chs. 22–24). These prophets, in fact,
had a precise though limited role. They played their part
in the cult of many a nation in the ancient world. They
were, to use a technical expression, 'enthuasiasts', that is

to say, men and women 'filled with God'; their frenzies, their speaking in tongues, their wild dances and their savage asceticisms were simply part of the liturgical process by which the god was invoked and his presence assured. They were regarded by the more sober members of society as 'mad fellows' and Saul, the first King of Israel, was, briefly at least, numbered amongst them (1 Samuel 10: 1–13). They operated in bands and called music to their aid (2 Kings 3:15). They were the 'Holy Rollers' of the pre-Christian era, with many successors in the Christian Church.

At a rather higher level of activity these prophets were often credited with powers of healing and enjoyed, as did Elijah and Elisha, a huge reputation amongst the people of the land. It was, after all, this particular aspect of our Lord's ministry in Galilee which first created an intense interest in him. If you want to be a serious student of the Bible you will have to disabuse yourself of some of the rationalist notions so popular at the beginning of this century. 'Miracles' are quite inseparable from the biblical narrative, and we shall have to get used to the idea that strange things happen which are not normally considered part of medical practice or of meteorology. The prophets, furthermore, found themselves often in great demand in the political and military fields. It would be possible to regard Elisha's healing of Naaman as a political act (2 Kings ch. 5). They were expected to be able to predict what the enemy would do, and Elisha proved a very able ally in this respect to the king in his wars with Syria (2 Kings 6: 8–12). We have grown more used in the nineteen-seventies to the notion that there are what we are pleased to call 'paranormal powers' available to human kind, which we once dismissed as witchcraft or magic. The prophets certainly had paranormal powers, and Saul was intending to make use of these powers when he was looking for the lost asses of his father. 'Walk up this track for five hundred cubits, turn left at the standing stone, climb the scree to the little copse at the top and you will find your lost asses sitting in the shade.' That would have been the kind of advice that Saul expected and he would have paid a modest fee for it.

We are still a long way from the great Prophets who are represented in the pages of Scripture but undoubtedly

these older elements are to be found in them and I think
therefore that it would be reasonable to suppose that the
Prophets did not spring fully-fledged from the mind of
God but had a history, a background, a milieu, a generally
recognised place in the official religions of the ancient
world. What we have to try to understand is how a
certain limited number of such men arose out of the ruck
to become spokesmen and leaders, theologians and
thinkers, poets and revolutionaries in one particular
official religion of the ancient world, that is, the religion
of Israel. For, to whatever extent the prophets have a
common pedigree, the fact remains that the great
Prophets of Israel, so far as we are aware, stand alone in
the history of religion. They rise dramatically from the
foothills of religion, great peaks of aspiration and
achievement upon which the sun shines for the comfort
and the delectation of us poor toilers here on the plain.
Savage winds blow around those mountain peaks and he is
an intrepid climber indeed who would want to share
the ardours of these great men. 'They suffered abuse and
isolation; they had trial of mockings and scourgings, of
bonds and imprisonment; they were stoned, they were
sawn asunder, they were tempted; they were slain with the
sword; they went about in sheepskins, in goatskins, being
destitute, afflicted, evil entreated, wandering in deserts
and mountains and caves and the holes of the earth. They
were strangers and pilgrims on the earth' (Hebrews 11).

What marked out these few great men living in a particular
period of Israelite history from their fellow prophets in the
lower echelons of their trade? Amos, at least, was quite
certain that he was marked out and makes the point that
he was 'no prophet nor a prophet's son' (Amos 7:14).
What were they then, and what were they trying to do?
If we may return to our earlier analogy, what was the cue
to which they so ardently responded, and what was the
message they had in common? They were obsessed – and
that is not too strong a word – with the reality and
universality of Yahweh, the God of Israel, and with the
special role which Israel had to play in the life of the world.
Both these beliefs are in fact very remarkable. The ancient
world was on the whole quite content with a diversity of
worship corresponding to a diversity of race and nation,
and never came to terms with the fierce Hebrew conviction
that there was only one God and that he was to be

worshipped without compromise. It was this theology that lay at the back of the famous incident on Mount Carmel where Elijah took issue with the prophets of Baal (1 Kings ch. 18). Marriage was then a regular vehicle of international co-operation and so it often happened that a queen from another nation would take her place in the court, bringing with her her own particular brand of religion, her own prophets and her own priests. To most of the nations of the ancient world this was a normally accepted practice which had advantages even outside the political scene, in so far as it ensured a wide range of religious aids for times of famine or war or seismic disturbance. There was safety in numbers. The great bulk of the Hebrew people themselves were perfectly happy with such an arrangement. That is why one has a sense that many of the kings of Israel were genuinely mystified by what would seem to them the fanaticism of the prophets, who insisted that there was only one God for Israel, indeed only one God for the world, and that he must be worshipped alone. So it came about that the prophets gave to the traditions of Israel, which were widely known and accepted – namely, the slavery in Egypt, the Exodus, the Wilderness, the entry into Canaan – a peculiar significance: i.e. that Israel was God's chosen people for the salvation of the world. I can offer only one explanation of this remarkable phenomenon, and the explanation is this – that it really was so. For reasons best known to himself, the Ruler of the Universe actually chose a little Middle-Eastern clan to become the vehicle of a particular revelation to all mankind. 'How odd of God to choose the Jews.'

We sometimes react against such a suggestion because it would seem to be gross favouritism on the part of the Deity; that is not how the prophets looked at it. To them, God's choice of a peculiar people imposed heavy and extremely unwelcome burdens upon that people and indeed upon themselves as the spokesmen of God, which they would have been glad to be rid of. The prophets did not rush on to the stage; they had to be pushed. Jeremiah would have been much happier with a walking-on part (Jeremiah 1:4–19). If indeed they were a peculiar people, then they could not be content with the standards and practices of the other nations. They were intended to be a light to lighten the Gentiles, and their social, corporate and religious life needed to bear the marks of their divine

origin and of their divine role in the history of the world.
It was for this reason that the prophets felt free to
criticise the religious institutions of their day, not because
they were institutions (as latter-day reformers would seem
to think) but because those institutions failed to live up to
the purpose for which they were created. The Temple was
perfectly acceptable as a house of prayer for all nations
but not as a device for making money, nor as a symbol of
power, nor as a citadel of privilege. The prophets did not
necessarily wish to do away with the cult, with the worship,
the services, the singing, the ritual, the holy books, the
priesthood, but they often looked at these activities with a
very jaundiced eye, seeing them as incidental to the great
role which God intended for Israel (Isaiah ch. 1). It is a
mistake to assume that God is interested only in religion,
and the prophets themselves would never have been
content with such a limited view. They took it upon
themselves to engage in politics, and had some very
pertinent and, as events turned out, wise things to say
about the relationships between Israel and the other nations
of the world, about treaties and trade-pacts. They looked
askance at the social life of their people and the commercial
and economic structures of their day, in which the rich
became richer and the poor became poorer (Amos 6), in
which profit was the only standard of success (Amos 8:5)
and in which inflation was rampant (Haggai 1:6). Their
attitudes were not simply the product of a humanitarian
concern but arose out of their deep conviction about a
holy God who had a plan for the world and who had laid
on his people the privilege and burden of making that
plan effective. My mind boggles at the daring and courage
of these ancient men of God, bearing in their own hearts
and uttering from their own lips this ineffable message for
mankind. The agonies of the whole world, not just of the
Jewish people, were pumped through the channels of their
hearts. Their physical sufferings, which were many, were as
nothing compared with the spiritual sufferings which they
endured in the interests of all humanity.

I was bold enough to say at the beginning of this book
that there is one theme running through all the pages of
the Old Testament and that theme is 'The Lord is King'.
If you doubted it then, I hope you will doubt it no longer.
It is the message of Deuteronomy and of the Torah, of
Psalms and Proverbs, the message, even in an obscure way,

of Ecclesiastes and Job; but it is the message par excellence of the prophets. The Lord is King of all the universe; the Lord is King of the Church; the Lord is King of the nations. The prophets were the real tigers, not the paper tigers of our modern revolutionary movements who imagine that all the problems will be solved when one regime is abolished and another put in its place; who make a commotion and mistake it for a miracle. Their unvarying message – that the Lord is King – is a revolutionary message calling not for a nice adjustment of political procedures nor for self-frustrating violence but for a revolution in inner attitudes towards God and towards men. They summoned the mighty of the land to make that change possible. They summoned the poor to inherit the Kingdom which God had prepared for them. The prophets are unique in the history of the world, the forerunners of him who in his own person represented the Kingdom of God and offered it to men. The prophets entered the holy place of God's presence every day, not just once a year, as the high priest was wont to do.

HIGHLIGHTS FROM THE PROPHETS

Isaiah 1:1–20
Isaiah 6:1–13
Isaiah 52:13–53:12
Jeremiah 1:1–19
Jeremiah 31:31–34
Ezekiel 37:1–28

Hosea 11:1–12
Amos 7:1–17
Micah 6:1–16
Habakkuk 3:17–19
Zechariah 8:1–17
Malachi 3:1–12

The prophets were not visionaries, content with the
ineffable vision of God for themselves and indifferent to
the world. They did not seek the vision of God, as the
mystics have sometimes done. They were confronted with
that vision and often reacted reluctantly to it. The story of
Isaiah's call is one of the most familiar in Holy Scripture
(Isaiah ch. 6) and perhaps the least well understood. The
vision came to him in the holiest place of all (the Temple)
at a time of acute anxiety in the nation, following the
death of that great and good King, Uzziah. The golden
era was over, the foundations of the national life were
trembling. So it was that Isaiah needed, and was given, an
assurance that the Lord was King, there was no cause to
fear – provided that the people remained faithful to him.
The rest of Isaiah's life was a protracted and often fruitless
attempt to procure that obedience. But it was not to any
vague concept of obedience (a kind of Lenten resolution)
to which Isaiah called his people, but to an obedience in
detail to the revealed will of God – and that will revealed
in the holiest place of all, namely, the Torah. There was
an opinion fashionable earlier this century that the law as
it was received in Israel was really the product of the
prophetic movement, a kind of codification of the prophetic
utterances. There is less support for that opinion now, and
I have never been able myself to share it. The biblical
tradition is surely the right one – not that the prophets
created the law, but rather that they appealed to a law
with which they and their people were already familiar.
Precisely what form the law took in the time of the
prophets we have no means of knowing. Law grows,
develops, changes – but we can be sure that it was a
version of the law that is articulated in the books we
now know as Exodus, Leviticus and Numbers.

In the grounds of the Holy Land Hotel in the suburbs of
Jerusalem the pilgrim will discover a large-scale model of
the city of Jerusalem as it was just before it fell in AD 70.
From each vantage-point round the model he will be given
a lecture in four languages on the public address system

and at one point will be introduced to the Temple – 'that snowy mountain', as Josephus said, 'glittering in the sun'. The Temple consisted of a series of Courts – the Court of the Gentiles, the Women's Court, the Court of the Israelites, the Inner Court, and finally at the heart of the whole edifice, the Sanctuary or the Holy of Holies, into which the High Priest went but once a year. This, if tradition is to be believed, used to contain the Tables of the Law given by the hand of Moses on Mount Sinai, together with other tokens of Israel's sojourn in the wilderness – the golden pot holding the manna, Aaron's rod that budded, and a golden censer. It is a striking fact, therefore, that the whole architectural edifice upon which the people of Israel lavished such care and labour and expense and the whole organisation of the priesthood and the cult which occupied so important a place in the life of Israel, were all centred on a box which contained two tablets of stone. For this the Hebrew people were prepared to live and to die with fanatical zeal. Even when surrounded by the Roman armies, with the battering rams drawing inexorably nearer, with famine and disease everywhere in the city, still the sacred ritual must go on, still the animals must be sacrificed before the ark of the covenant in which the two tablets of stone were preserved.

The architecture of the Temple has its equivalent in the architecture of the Old Testament. The equivalent to the Holy of Holies on the hill of Zion is that section of the book of Exodus from chapter 19 to chapter 32 which contains the account of the giving of the Law. Everything before it leads up to that point, everything after is to be regarded either as the consequence of that mighty act or as a commentary upon it. You will never understand the Jewish people or their Scriptures unless you take account of the intense devotion which through centuries of their history they have given to this holy of holies, the Torah, the Teaching – and it is to this subtle, penetrating, architectonic book that we shall now give our attention.

I exclude from this chapter and defer until later a discussion of Genesis. I shall exclude also the book of Deuteronomy, having already after a fashion dealt with it in an earlier chapter. We shall, therefore, be concentrating exclusively on the series of events which led to the giving of the Law, and produced the conviction in the Hebrew mind that this Law was not the product of some primitive parliament legislating for the good of society but the work of God himself. As the writer of Exodus puts it, 'the tables were the work of God and the writing was the writing of God' – you could not have it plainer than that. But this is an extraordinary assertion when you realise that the author would have been perfectly well aware of other codes of law obtaining in other parts of the Near East, for which no such claims were made (see Appendix 4). He is saying, in so many words, that the Hebrew people were chosen of God to be the recipients of a law not simply for themselves but, in so far as their God was God of the whole earth, for all mankind. He is making universal claims for a law which was given to this little group of nomads en route from Egypt to Canaan. This kind of claim is like a detonator in the Western mind, which on the whole prefers a philosophy of history more rational, less exclusive, more accommodating. But the proper question to ask is not, 'Can we believe it?' but, 'Can it be true?' The question presses upon our attention; we cannot ignore it. If it is true, it changes our whole attitude to life; we are to understand ourselves not as seekers after truth but as recipients of a truth which we may or may not choose to accept, the truth being that Yahweh, the God of the Hebrews, is the God of the whole earth; that he has made his will known through his chosen people and that in the knowledge of his will is our peace. We are not looking for a formula for a happy society; we already have it.

Before we can be expected to take such a claim seriously we must have some confidence in the documents which support it, and here I must trespass on your patience and try to describe the process by which these documents reached the form in which we now have them (see Appendix 3). It goes without saying that any such an attempt is bound to be tentative because we do not have access to the original documents. The documents we have are the consequence of many centuries of copying and recopying, of emendation and editing, of collection and comment. But over the last hundred years there has grown up a measure of agreement about the constituent parts of the documents that we are considering. Whoever was responsible for the final form of the Pentateuch, he did not write history out of the top of his head (and I am glad he

did not); he gathered his source material; put in editorial
comments where necessary; arranged it in what he took
to be the right order and only occasionally bothered to
acknowledge his sources. The ancient world did not use
quotation marks and authors had no rights. It goes without
saying, therefore, that a document which took perhaps a
thousand years to reach its present form is bound to be
composite. The usual hypothesis is that the Pentateuch
was composed of four main elements. The first (in academic
shorthand) is the J code, believed to have been recorded in
the Southern Kingdom of Judah, which uses by preference
the name 'Yahweh' as the name of God. It probably dates
from the early part of the monarchy. The second code has
been called E and uses 'Elohim' as the divine name. It
probably originated in Ephraim, the Northern Kingdom,
and dates from slightly later. The third element is called
D, which is shorthand for the Deuteronomist, whose
presence we have already discerned in the prophetic
writings. The fourth main element is called P, standing for
the priestly writers of the exilic and post-exilic period who
were responsible for unifying the whole corpus of literature
and imparting to it their own particular view of its meaning
(see Appendix 3). The only serious argument about these
sources now is whether these letters correspond to any
particular written source or whether they represent certain
oral traditions in the life of Israel. For the ordinary reader
of the Pentateuch I doubt whether this is a very significant
issue. What is significant, however, is that whether these
sources were written or oral they all agree in basing the
life of their people upon a series of events which began
with the call of Moses and culminated, but did not end,
with the giving of the Law at Sinai. This is why I find that
the documentary criticism of the last two or three hundred
years, far from destroying the value of the Bible, has
enormously enhanced it. Its authority does not rest upon
the genius of a single man but rather upon a synoptic
view of the history of Israel to which many different
writers at many different times have contributed. It is the
sheer unanimity of these writers which impresses me. Of
this one thing at least we can be assured – we have a
document in front of us which springs out of and is part
of history. It was written by real people with the writing
materials of their particular age; it has, so far as we are
able to gather, been transmitted with commendable
fidelity down the centuries. If I may say so in passing,

part of the importance of the discoveries at Qumran is that they show with what fidelity the text has been transmitted. The Massoretic text, dating from the eighth century AD, is not all that much different from the texts which were discovered at Qumran dating from the first or second century BC! We are therefore in the presence of a reliable tradition – but did anything really happen?

Did anything really happen? With certain qualifications the answer must be 'yes', the qualifications being that the events described were a long way off in history from the person describing them and that there are bound to be contradictions, misunderstandings, duplications and even slips of the pen. But the event itself is no longer seriously disputed. If Moses did not exist we would have to invent him; for someone took hold of a dispirited, enslaved people in Egypt, brought them out into the wilderness, led them for forty years by a devious route and in the process received a Law, called the Decalogue, which in the process of years was elaborated into the body of law which we have in Exodus, Leviticus and Numbers. It was on the basis of this law that the civic life of Israel was conducted; it was this law which formed the basis of constitutional government and it was this law to which the prophets incessantly appealed. The existence of the Jewish synagogue in your town, or the Christian church in your street, is a contemporary witness to the fact that something happened. But what happened?

To their neighbours in the Near East (the Moabites, the Edomites, the Philistines, the Jebuzites, the Hittites, the Syrians) the Hebrew people were no more than a marauding group characterised by strange religious customs and fearsome fanaticism, who were striving to escape from the nomadic life and make a home for themselves in Canaan. Near-Eastern history over the centuries has been full of the records of such groups, seeking to establish themselves in the Fertile Crescent. Most of them came, imposed a momentary authority – and then disappeared into the mists of history. But in the synagogue in your home town there will be people worshipping every Saturday who are the direct descendants of one of those wild groups who struck terror into the hearts of their neighbours, razed their cities, trampled on their crops, and put their menfolk to the sword. You may not observe the lineaments of their

history in the quiet, good-natured citizens in dark suits
who go down your street to the synagogue but they are
the sons and daughters of ancient Israel, recipients of the
Law of God. We of the Christian Church are, after the
flesh, Gentiles but we too are spiritually descendants of
ancient Israel. We are kinsmen who pass each other on
the pavement from Monday to Friday but kinsmen
separated by a high wall of partition on Saturday and
Sunday.

'How odd of God to choose the Jews'. And yet this is the
message of Old Testament and New Testament alike.
We are confronted with a conviction which has endured
through the tragedies and accidents of history to our own
time, that they hold in trust for the world a law which
represents the mind of God and which it is man's duty and
man's joy to obey. Man's joy? This is perhaps not the
picture which is presented to us by orthodox Jewry's
painstaking attention to what appears to us trivial customs
of dress, of diet and of ritual. On our side of the partition,
furthermore, we have grown accustomed to the powerful
diatribes of St. Paul as he rails against the Jewish legalism
of his day. But that is to misunderstand the issue. Beneath
the elaborations and accretions of time, there is, so the Jews
would say, a hard deposit of revealed truth and that
revealed truth finds expression in the ten 'words' recorded
in stone in the box, in the Temple, in the Holy of Holies.
Take for example just one of the Ten Commandments –
'Thou shalt not covet'. It is a long way from the Sinai
Desert to Bond Street and the advertising agency and the
television commercial, to the competing interests in the
North Sea and to the struggles for power in the Middle
East, but over them all hangs the judgement represented
by that authoritative word, 'Thou shalt not covet'. On
that view of the matter, the covetous, acquisitive modern
society is an affront to God's law. The Jewish believer at
his best did not find the Law a burden; he rejoiced in it
because in its observance he found peace in his own heart,
a persuasive rule of life for himself and a formula (the only
one) for establishing humane and lasting relationships.
It is no good reading the Torah, or indeed any part of
the Old Testament, as if it were just a prelude to the
New; nor as if it were simply of antiquarian interest, or a
useful aid to private devotion. We can only read the Old
Testament in the spirit in which it was written, taking

seriously the claim that the Lord of the Hebrews is the Lord of all the earth and we are to love the Lord, the God of the Hebrews, with all our heart and mind and soul and strength. There are times when my own mind reels at the implications of that astonishing claim. Like Augustine, if in this respect only, 'I believe because it is impossible'.

NOTABLE PASSAGES

Exodus 3:1-4:17
Exodus 7-11
Exodus 12:1-13:16
Exodus 19 and 20
Exodus 32

Numbers 13:16-15:5
Leviticus 16 (Day of
  Atonement)
Leviticus 19 (Holiness)

11 The rise of Judaism
Chronicles, Ezra, Nehemiah

You may have noticed that most of the literature we have been handling achieved the form in which we now have it some time after the Exile (see Appendix 3). This is not altogether surprising; when nations are winning wars and extending their empires, they have little time for reflection and sometimes no taste for it. It tends to be when the imperial role declines that literature begins and George Orwell of the Burma Police becomes George Orwell the novelist. That is not quite such an outrageous comparison as it might seem. Like George Orwell, the thinkers and writers of the post-exilic period were having to reflect upon that history which they had hitherto taken for granted and find some explanation for the political disintegration which had overtaken them. I ask you to imagine what the effect would have been upon our own nation, if in one disastrous night of the blitz Canterbury Cathedral, Westminster Abbey, York Minster, the Houses of Parliament and Buckingham Palace had all gone up in flames, taking in the latter case the whole of the Royal Family with it. Even in a nation not renowned for its godliness or its unthinking devotion to monarchy, or its regard for politicians, there would have been a certain sense of loss, an awareness that something had gone which could never be replaced. But that is a pale analogy for the fate that had overtaken Israel. They had believed that they were the chosen of God, with a permanent and indispensable role to play in the world. The Northern Kingdom had already fallen one hundred and fifty years before but the remnant of Israel continued to bolster themselves up with the knowledge that Jerusalem still stood and the sacred services were still conducted in the Temple. Now, it seemed, their identity as a nation was totally lost. What were they to make then of their chosenness? And what about the monarchy, that repository of all the ancient hopes and aspirations of the people, around which the national life had revolved and by which in the end the rule of God was to be introduced? There was no Son of David any more on the throne of Judah.

The reaction to the disaster of 587 took a variety of forms
in the years that followed it. The first is represented by the
Wisdom writings, which largely date from this period. They
provided a legitimate means by which individual men and
women came to terms with the loss of their national
identity, and developed a more personal and individual
view of life not entirely dependent upon their membership
of the chosen community. They were 'westernised'; they
addressed themselves not to the fate of the nation but to
the dread questions of personal existence in a hostile
universe. There is not much about politics or international
policy in the books of Ecclesiastes and Job.

The second reaction and a less obvious one is reflected
in the so-called 'Former Prophets', the books of 1/2
Samuel and 1/2 Kings. The prophet, with his acute
awareness of the nation as the chosen of God and his
concern for its political and social life, could hardly be
expected to follow the Wisdom line. Somehow there must
be another explanation for the appalling fate which had
overtaken the Davidic dynasty. The prophets' answer was
to be found in the way in which they handled the history
of that dynasty. It was easy to see that the later members of
the Davidic dynasty had not maintained the traditions of
David their ancestor and had not secured obedience to
God's revealed Law either in their own lives or in the
conduct of national policy. The fall of Jerusalem, therefore,
could be seen as divine judgement, such as they had
forecast, upon an apostate king and an apostate nation.
This did not mean, however, that God's purposes for
Israel were thereby frustrated. The institution of the
monarchy, as is made clear by the diverse accounts in 1
Samuel, was an ambiguous act. The people had demanded
it in order that they might be like the other nations. God
had acceded to their demand, but this was essentially an
interim institution; the real King of Israel was Yahweh
himself and he did not cease to be King when the capital
of David fell. The point is perfectly made in the familiar
passage of Isaiah chapter 6. 'When King Uzziah died', so it
says, 'Isaiah saw the Lord high and lifted up and his train
filled the Temple.' Uzziah had been a great and good king
and his death produced tremors in the body politic of
Israel but (this is Isaiah's message) the Lord was King
and he still reigned. The prophetic writers by no means
despaired of monarchy as an institution, but looked for

that time when another Son of David would reign in
power and justice and mercy, as the vice-regent of God,
and when not only Israel but the whole world would
obey him. This Messianic view of the future does not
depend upon a text here and a text there; it is implicit in
the whole message of 1/2 Samuel and 1/2 Kings and
permeates the whole of the author's work. His theology,
his understanding of his people's role in the world. his
hope for the future, all depended on the coming of another
David, the anointed of the Lord. But for people of a
certain cast of mind, these dim longings for and assurances
about the ultimate future of the nation were not enough
and there is a certain section of the third Canon (the
Writings) which reflects another kind of reaction to the
events of 587. It is to these books, Chronicles, Ezra and
Nehemiah that we now turn.

The literary and historical problems in this section are
many and they are probably insoluble. The most obvious
problem is that in the Hebrew Bible the book of Chronicles
comes right at the end preceded by Ezra and Nehemiah,
which should logically come after it (see Appendix 2).
That this was so in our Lord's time is evident from
Matthew 23:34–35 which you may consult for yourself.
There is no conclusive explanation for this curious
phenomenon but the most likely one is that the books
Ezra and Nehemiah originally circulated on their own and
found an accepted place in Hebrew literature to be followed
later by the books of Chronicles. This would account
for the fact that the end of the second book of Chronicles
is repeated at the beginning of Ezra (2 Chronicles 36:22,
23 – Ezra 1:1–3).

The second insoluble problem relates to the relationship
between Ezra and Nehemiah. The traditional view is that
Ezra arrived in Jerusalem in 458 BC in the reign of
Artaxerxes I and Nehemiah followed him. A more recent
theory holds that Ezra arrived in 428, which means that
Nehemiah preceded him. This is a matter which has
exercised the minds of scholars over many years and
exasperated many of their pupils, but there seems no
means of resolving the issue. The only thing we can be
certain of is that the whole corpus of literature which we
call 1 and 2 Chronicles, Ezra and Nehemiah has a literary
unity of its own which embraces original source-material

(the memoirs of Ezra and the memoirs of Nehemiah)
and takes over-all a consistent view of the history of
Israel and in particular of the events which overtook
Israel in that fateful year of 587 BC.

I have already said that it is of the utmost importance to
try to establish the date and authorship of any book you
study. All that we can say with certainty in this case is
that the final form of Chronicles-Ezra-Nehemiah must
date from after the last event recorded within it or after
the date of the last known person in the genealogies which
the Chronicler so lavishly supplies. A date of about 250
BC satisfies these conditions and is borne out in some
degree by the style of the Hebrew and the vocabulary of
the writer. This, however, is not as helpful as it might
be to the understanding of the book because it is possible
that the book took various forms over a period of centuries
and that the final author may just have worked over a
much earlier work, simply adding information which was
accessible only to him. The permutations on this theme are
endless. Is it possible, therefore, to say something useful
about authorship? The author was, in the view of one
Old Testament scholar, 'A devotee to his music; an
accomplished statistician and an enthusiast for the ideals
of his order. He may well be compared to some monkish
historian of the middle ages, viewing life through the
tinted windows of the cloister and fired with the ambition
to turn to account the lessons of the past as a means to
lead men to God. His one disqualification for the work of
an historian was the absoluteness of his devotion to the
Levitical ideals, with the consequent tendency to read back
the conditions of his own day into the remote past and to
judge an earlier age as though its standards and attainments
were identical with his own.' That is well said, and would
certainly be true of large sections of the work. No man is
going to attempt a history of Israel unless he is to some
extent and for some reason dissatisfied with the histories
which already exist. We may presume that the author of
Chronicles was familiar with the books of Samuel and
Kings but he is obviously not content with the message –
or perhaps he does not understand it. For him the demise
of the Davidic monarchy is not just a sign of the judgement
of God upon an apostate nation, nor a challenge to
recapture the former vision of the Lord as King of Israel.
Good churchman as he was, he saw the role of the

monarchy as primarily an ecclesiastical one; that is why
presumably he attributes to David an interest in the
Temple, the liturgy and the priesthood which, if the
author of 1/2 Samuel is to be believed, did not dominate
David's mind to the extent that the Chronicler would have
us believe. His aim is to show that the monarchy was
instituted specifically to establish on the Hill of Zion a
Temple in which the really serious business of life could
go on. Not for the Chronicler the din of battle, or
international politics or a concern with social ethics, but
the orderly organisation of the priesthood and the regular
offering of the sacrifice. Similar views are not unknown
in the Church of our day. The collapse of the Davidic
dynasty was not, therefore, the total disaster that it
appeared; the purpose for which it was created had been
achieved; atonement for the sins of the holy people was
regularly being procured upon the holy mount.

It would be nice if we could rest content with such a tidy
theory but the material of 1/2 Chronicles, Ezra and
Nehemiah will not be entirely forced into this theological
strait-jacket. The books also reflect a process by which
after the Exile the centre of gravity moved away from the
prophet and the priest. Ezra revived the great Mosaic
ideal of the Law of God as the regulator of Hebrew life
but he did more than that – he was responsible for the
movement which created that painstaking but pedantic
devotion to the letter of the Law which came to be so
characteristic of the Judaism of our Lord's day. It is not
the priest in front of the altar in the Temple who presides
over the history of post-exilic Judaism but the scribe and
the doctor of the law, the rabbi and the synagogue teacher.
Ezra was a scribe, not a priest. This was, I suppose,
inevitable given the actual situation of the Hebrews. Only
a tiny proportion of them still lived in Judah; the rest were
scattered up and down the Mediterranean and in
Mesopotamia, conducting their own business, maintaining
their national identity and adhering faithfully to their only
possession. They had no temple, no prophet, no priest, no
king, but they did have a book. They became the people
of a book and that book the Torah, as it was developed in
the labyrinthine minds of the casuist and the lawyer. The
rebuilding of the wall by Nehemiah and the re-enactment
of the Law by Ezra, important though these were in the
short term, were nothing like as important in the long

term as the building of the spiritual wall around the
innumerable Jewish communities which lived out their
lives in the great concrete cities of their day. The
Judaism with which you may be familiar in your
neighbourhood is the Judaism of Ezra, not necessarily of
David or of the Prophets or even of Moses. I used to be
rather proud of the apophthegm that I gave to my students
in Oxford – 'Nehemiah's walls constituted the tomb of
prophecy and Ezra's law its obituary.' It is not entirely
true but it is true enough to be uncomfortable.

It is a memorable experience to walk through the quarter
of Jerusalem known as Mea Shearim on the eve of the
Sabbath. The women and children will be there, gaily
dressed, walking in the narrow streets of that quarter,
engaged in animated conversation, waiting for the men to
return from the synagogue service. Synagogue did I say?
No, dozens of synagogues, ministering to Jews of every
nation and every tongue, who over the centuries have
gathered together in that place – Russians, Poles, Lithuanians,
Germans, French, Spanish, Morroccan, all in their
traditional dress, holding fast to their traditional customs
but united by one thing – their total devotion to the Torah
as it is understood and expounded in the synagogue. It is
an impressive sight. The barriers which the police put up
all round that quarter for the Sabbath are an indication,
even within the state of Israel itself, of the ghetto-complex
which has sometimes afflicted the Jewish people. It is the
rabbi who reigns supreme – not the priest, nor the prophet
and certainly not the government – proposing to his
people survival, isolation, purity, superiority to all
mankind on the basis of exact adherence to the Law. A
walk through Mea Shearim on Sabbath eve is an impressive
but not a particularly encouraging experience; the spirit
of Ezra broods over it still. It is distinctly not 'for all
mankind'.

NOTABLE PASSAGES

2 Chronicles 34   Nehemiah 2:11–18
Ezra 9:1–15   Nehemiah 4:16–23

12 The flight from the world
Daniel

To stand amongst the ruins of Khirbet Qumran in the early morning and to crawl along the aqueduct which originally brought water to that thriving community, is to enter a new and unfamiliar world. It is true that there was a settlement there as early as the eighth century BC but it was the discovery of the scrolls in the nearby caves in the year 1947 which led to the excavation of the more modern settlement dating from the reign of John Hyrcanus at the end of the second century BC. From our point of view the existence of the settlement and the evidence which it has supplied is even more important than the earlier discovery of the scrolls associated with it. By whatever name the sect might properly be known – and that is still a matter of dispute – there is no doubt that it represents a highly sophisticated theological viewpoint and illustrates for us the direction which Jewish history took in the period after the Exile. This period is of the utmost significance for our understanding of the Scriptures because the bulk of them took their final shape within it (see Appendix 3). It is also of special significance to the Christian because it was the immediate prelude to the coming of John the Baptist and the birth of Christ. One of the weaknesses of Bible study up to this century has been its preoccupation with the pre-exilic period and an almost total indifference to the developments in Judaism in the five centuries before Christ. To put it more succinctly, our approach has been disproportionately biblicist, based rather on what was being described in the histories and prophecies of the Old Testament than on who was describing it. We need to understand, for example, the process by which the books of the Old Testament came to be differentiated from the rest of Israel's literary heritage for use in temple and synagogue. We need to know about the religious and cultural background of those who presided over this process and ultimately produced what we call the 'Canon of Scripture' at the 'Council' of Jamnia around AD 90.

But what has this to do with Daniel? The book of Daniel

itself is as mysterious a production as the prophecies which
constitute part of it. It is, for example, one of the few
documents in the Bible where Aramaic is used extensively.
So the book begins in Hebrew and goes down as far as
chapter 2 verse 4, where (understandably because it is the
Chaldeans who are speaking) the section in Aramaic begins.
The Aramaic continues until chapter 7 verse 28 and
Hebrew begins again at the beginning of chapter 8, and
continues to the end. Most of the explanations for this
phenomenon are far from convincing. I mention one of
them – that the book was originally written in Aramaic
throughout but at some stage a scribe translated the
earlier and latter parts into Hebrew in order to make it
more 'respectable' for synagogue reading. This to my taste
is altogether too artificial an explanation. I prefer my own
and it is this. The book, as befits the work of a fervent
nationalist, begins in the patriotic tongue of his own day
but once the Chaldeans begin to speak it must change
naturally to Syrian or Aramaic and it would seem reasonably
natural to maintain that language until the end of that
section. My own feeling is that in fact the book of Daniel
circulated in two halves, the first one in Aramaic for the
greater part, ending, as indeed it suggests, at 7:28; this is
written in the third person by an unknown author about
Daniel. The book which begins at chapter 8 is entirely
composed of Daniel's visions and is written in the first
person; the author, however, making it perfectly clear that
he wishes to associate this section with the earlier section
by using the words, 'A vision appeared unto me, even to
me, Daniel'. In so far as these visions were exclusively the
visions of Daniel, there was no reason why they should not
be written in the language of Daniel, that is in Hebrew.

The second puzzling feature is that the document is not
included amongst the Prophets but amongst the Writings.
Why did the Jewish people relegate it to the Writings,
which is division three in the league by any standards?
There are only two convincing explanations: either it was
felt by the Rabbis of the pre-Christian era that this book
was not prophetic in style or content, or that the second
division of the Canon had already been widely accepted
and the Canon closed. I ask you to imagine how difficult
it would be, for example, after centuries of its use in the
sacred liturgies of the Church, if someone should propose
the addition of another book to the Bible. It might be a

good book but custom and liturgy could not make room for it. So there the book stands amongst the sacred Writings, interesting and edifying for those who wish to use it but with no 'authority' in the Jewish Church.

I hope you will not resent it if I remind you once more of a highly important principle behind the Sacred Scriptures. It is necessary to give your attention not only to the content of a book but to ask yourself the question – What kind of person wrote it and with what purpose? No claim is made that a man Daniel wrote this book. Daniel is spoken of in the opening verses in the third person. He is no more likely to have written it than Hananiah or Mishael. We shall never know the name of the man who wrote it, but it is possible to make certain propositions regarding the kind of person who wrote it and why. Daniel saw a vision, it says, of four enormous beasts coming out of the stormy Mediterranean, each different from the others. Most scholars are of the opinion that the four beasts stand for four great kingdoms or civilisations: the first Assyrian, the second Babylonian, the third Persian and the fourth Greek. If that is so then it must have been written after Alexander's conquest in 333 BC and comes from a period when the Jewish faith and customs were under heavy pressure from the Greek-style civilisation in which they lived.

It needs to be understood that Alexander the Greek was not just a conqueror, with his father's flair for military strategy. He was a missionary and an evangelist, believing that in the Greek style of life, in Greek literature, culture and philosophy, lay the salvation of the world (see Appendix 4). Any visitor to Israel will find evidences before him wherever he turns of the pervasive influence of Greek civilisation in this period – the remnants of the hippodrome at Caesarea, theatres, foreign-style illustrations on the floors of ancient synagogues, references to Greek customs and the presence of Greek words in the everyday language of the Jews. This penetration by Greek culture was a far more dangerous and insidious attack upon the Jewish faith than any which had been launched by the great conquerors of the past. This fourth beast was, as the book says, terrifying and powerful, had great teeth of iron and the power to trample things under foot. But that was only to the eyes of orthodoxy. To the eyes of the average

Jewish youngster growing up in a Greek city it had a very pleasing aspect; it offered an entrance to culture and learning, to prosperity and government service. It offered a welcome release from the stuffy habits and trivial regulations which his parents sought to impose. Greek civilisation, as it was expressed outside Greece itself, was the pop-culture of the day. It was one of the wild beasts which surrounded our Lord at his Temptation, every bit as powerful in his day as in the day of the writer of the book of Daniel. The author's purpose, therefore, is to rally the troops against this insidious invader. It was to show how one man at least (Daniel), surrounded by the sophisticated attractions of Babylon, held firm to his faith, observed the dietary laws, maintained the regular hours for prayer and was rewarded with God's favour. Viewed in that light it is a magnificent tract for the times, fit to take its place with many another tract which has sufficed to steady the nerves of a fearful nation or a seemingly dying church. Daniel in the lions' den not only closed the lions' mouths but silenced the siren voices which had summoned many unsuspecting victims in his nation to their doom.

So far so good, but what are we to make of the second section of the book beginning with chapter 8, in which we enter a world, mysterious and melodramatic, of which we have little experience within the other pages of Scripture? Back to Qumran and the ruins of that ancient settlement on the banks of the Dead Sea, with its tower, its refectory, its scriptorium, its assembly hall, its potter's workshop, its baptistries, and the elaborate water system which made life possible there at all in that burning sulphurous heat. In the previous chapters we have seen two alternative reactions to the disaster which overtook Judah in 587. The Prophets on the whole contented themselves with the conviction that Yahweh was King and that ultimately someone of David's line would rule as his vice-regent, bringing new life and independence and national identity back to his people. The Chronicler, with a distinctly smaller horizon, saw the salvation of his people preserved in the life of the Temple or subsequently in the life of the synagogue and the devotion to the Law which went with it. The one dreamed of a distant spiritual empire, the other of a beleaguered people, surrounded by the walls of habit and custom, clinging desperately to the traditions which they had received, putting up 'no traffic' signs on the

Sabbath day against even the less orthodox of their own kindred.

There was, however, another way of looking at the disaster of 587 and that way is represented by the community at Qumran and communities like it which sprang up notably during the Greek period. These communities comprised groups of orthodox Jews who despaired of the world, saw no signs of the spiritual empire after which the Prophets longed and observed how inroads were being made by Greek culture and civilisation through the ramparts of Jewish orthodoxy. For them there was only one way of salvation and that was to remove themselves physically from the temptations by which they were assailed and establish the ideal community as they imagined it to be in places remote from human habitation and hostile to human civilisation. Khirbet Qumran fulfilled both these conditions – and more. I can do no more than introduce you to the distinctive writings of this sect. They are marked by a strong sense of vocation amongst the community itself, a willing subjection to formidable disciplines of body, mind and spirit, and a fervent longing for the intervention from on high which would set all things to rights and establish the God of the Universe on his proper throne. You will find the same emphases in the book of Daniel. Read it and test it for yourself – the same bitter distaste for the manners of the world, whether it be Assyrian, Babylonian or Greek; the same insistence on minute obedience to the Law; the same heroic spirituality which left little room for the natural pieties and the same prevailing vision of one who was 'to come on the clouds of heaven like unto a Son of Man, to whom would be given dominion and glory and a kingdom that all peoples, nations and languages should serve him'. This is normally called the apocalyptic view of life, to be found also within the pages of the New Testament, notably in the Apocalypse (or Revelation) which has many theological and literary affinities with the book of Daniel. For all its greatness and the heroism that it engenders amongst its adherents – no one could have been braver than Daniel or the unknown members of that community by the Dead Sea – it is essentially a cry of despair. It springs from a feeling that the rulers of the world are having it all their own way and that God is a long way off. It engenders not only heroism, it engenders that kind of spirituality which is so

characteristic of the book of Daniel, in which God takes
on the aspect of an oriental king, remote, unpredictable, to
be approached only with the greatest concern for protocol;
who honours you, may be, with his attention but does not
take you in a loving embrace.

History did not stop at the end of BC and start again at the
beginning of AD. We remain inheritors, whether we
recognise it or not, of that old conflict in the heart between
the attractions of the world (some of them perfectly
legitimate) and the demands of the spirit, which may issue
on the one hand in the loving reverie of a son with his
father or on the other hand in a certain kind of bigotry
which finds salvation only in the burning wastes of
Qumran or the lions' den in Babylon. I have never myself
been able to come to terms altogether with this dilemma.
Read the book of Daniel and the Gospel according to St.
Luke alongside each other and you will at least perceive
the dilemma, even if you are unable to resolve it.

To complete our work on the Writings we would have to
include Ruth, Esther, the Song of Solomon and
Lamentations, but enough has been said to show how
diverse the Writings are. The urbane cynicism of
Ecclesiastes is far removed from the fervent fanaticism of
the Qumran Sect or a latter-day Daniel. The banal
sentiments of the Proverbs would have grated
disconcertingly on the ears of that great religious man, the
author of the book of Job. The Chronicler's preoccupation
with cult and law would have provoked no answering
response in the heart of the Psalmist wrestling with his
God. It is this variety that I would press upon your
attention. These Writings, without exception, come from
the post-exilic period, that period in the life of Israel which
leads up to the coming of Christ. We need to understand
that the Jewish religion of that period was a strange
amalgam (and at times hardly even that) of theologies
apparently at variance with each other, of attitudes to the
world utterly distinct, of hopes for the future which must
appear to anything but the most penetrating mind utterly
contradictory to each other. Jesus of Nazareth was born
into a real world, facing in his own person opposing views
of the world and of history and of God, which were
tearing his people apart. You will never understand the
New Testament unless you learn to detect behind it the

shadowy but powerful figures of the rabbi in his synagogue, of the priest at his altar, of the scribe in his scriptorium on the banks of the Dead Sea and of the latter-day Daniel in his lions' den.

NOTABLE PASSAGES

Daniel 3
Daniel 5

13 A missionary manifesto
Jonah

'My God, this is an awesome place,
  Without coal or candle;
With only fishes' tripes to eat
  And fishes' tripes to handle.'

So, believe it or not, runs the opening verse of a hymn
(based on the book of Jonah) which until comparatively
recently maintained its place in a highly reputable collection
of hymns and was sung with great sincerity, though perhaps
with little understanding, in the churches of this land. It
is just one of the perils of authorship that a book should
be so palpably misunderstood, and sad for us all that a
book with a humane and distinctive message for mankind
should have been a battleground upon which literalists and
liberals fought their meaningless and inconclusive battles.
It is nowhere more important than here to ask those
questions which I have pressed upon you throughout –
'What sort of book is it?' 'What sort of person wrote it?'
'When and Why?' The format is unique in the Old
Testament; it consists of a simple and apparently artless
narrative about a certain prophet named Jonah who
(according to 2 Kings ch. 14) lived at Gath-hepher in
Galilee. Little else is known about him. The narrative
includes a psalm. The message of the prophet, which in
other cases dominates the prophetic books, is brief. It
must be the shortest sermon in history – 'Yet forty days
and Nineveh shall be overthrown'. Moreover, whereas
the Prophets spoke exclusively to the church, to their own
people, Jonah is alone in speaking to a heathen people,
the people of Nineveh. Whereas the Prophets were
reformers, calling for spiritual renewal, Jonah is an
evangelist, calling for repentance and faith.

It is easy to overstate the contrasts and I would not
wish to prejudice your minds, but I think you will see that
there is a marked difference between the format of Jonah
and of the other Prophets in the collection. Yet the
remarkable fact is that the book of Jonah is included in
the Canon of the Prophets, whereas the book of Daniel,
which approximates more nearly to the prophetic pattern,

is excluded. We do not know who wrote the book, for it
is written in the third person about Jonah, not in the first
person by Jonah. We cannot be sure when it was written
because the language and the vocabulary offer no clue and
the historical allusions are too slight to be of any value.
The writer either quotes or is quoted by the author of the
book of Joel and if we were sure which way round that
was, we could have a guess at the date. All I think we can
be certain about is that it is in the post-exilic period and is
written by someone who at least shared the old prophetic
view of the world and of the church, though in one
instance departing radically from it. You may, however, be
comforted to know that we can speak with more confidence
about why he wrote it – but to do so we shall have to try
to understand more of the background against which he
wrote, the milieu out of which he spoke.

We have seen that Hebrew history and thought moves in
a kind of ellipse around two focal points, the one the
establishment of the Hebrew Kingdom under David and
the other the demise of the Hebrew Kingdom in the
catastrophe of 587 BC. The documents of the post-exilic
period return to this theme over and over again because,
as we have seen, the collapse of Jerusalem in 587 and the
destruction of the Temple, constituted a serious challenge
not only to the reality of Israel's vocation to be the
Chosen People but also to their convictions about the
providence and purpose of God in history, upon which
their whole theology was built. It has been fashionable at
some periods in the Church's history to decry the
importance of theology. The authors of the Old
Testament did not make this mistake. Unless they could
establish the role of Israel within the purposes of God –
that is, unless they had a convincing theology – they could
not survive, except as a little sect clinging blindly to the
past and maintaining their institutions for the sake of
maintaining them. Various answers were essayed as we have
seen: the prophetic answer that because Yahweh was King
and ultimately would reign, the people of Israel need not
feel too disconsolate about the loss of their earthly king;
the Chronicler's answer that the monarchy had been raised
up of God to create the Temple and the worship and the
sacred priesthood and this having been done the monarchy
was no longer indispensable; the apocalyptic answer
represented in the book of Daniel that the people of Israel

could not look for the renewal of the world but only that
far-off divine event by which history should be rolled up
and God reign in his glory, ineffable and unmediated. It
was the author of the book of Jonah, following perhaps
in the steps of his great predecessor responsible for the
central section of the book of the prophet Isaiah, who
struck a more challenging and at the same time more
hopeful note, which gave back to the people of Israel a
proper conception of their role in history and of their
responsibility to the world. For Jonah it was not sufficient
that Israel should live in its ghetto, under its gourd,
sheltered from the midday sun, meditating upon the Law
and leaving it at that. They had a responsibility for the
great secular cities of their day; for the arrogant civilisations
by which they were surrounded; for the poor benighted
Gentiles amongst whom they lived and who did not know
their right hand from their left. It is a book of astonishing
compassion for the world, not matched until we get to the
pages of the New Testament where our Lord spoke in
similar terms of the responsibility of the Church to preach
the Gospel to the world. 'Go, teach all nations' is the
message of the author of Jonah and of the author of the
Gospel according to St. Matthew. But why this elaborate
form for so simple a message?

We who live in the twentieth century, whose ears and eyes
are daily assaulted by crude words and crude symbols,
sometimes overlook the extreme sensitivity and subtlety
of the authors of this ancient literature we have been
studying. Not for them the clumsy tract thrusting the
author's opinions down his victim's throat; not for them
the heavy headline and the exclamation marks, but rather
the seemingly artless tale about a person whose name would
immediately command attention in the circles for which he
wrote – and within that artless tale a powerful blow at
the accepted religious attitudes of his day. Bunyan did it,
William Law did it and so did George MacDonald and
Charles Williams and C. S. Lewis. We do not demand the
exact measurements of 'yon wicket gate' nor ask how many
bars it had or what colour it was painted. Questions about
the size of the great fish and improving stories about
sailors who suffered the same fate as the prophet Jonah
do not help to elucidate the message. For the great fish
is a well-known symbol for Babylon, swallowing up captive
peoples and regurgitating them in alien lands. Even the

name Jonah means 'dove', which is a symbol for Israel.
So the message is plain – the people of Israel are not to
look back upon 587 simply as a disaster but to see it
rather as an opportunity for preaching the Gospel to the
peoples amongst whom they now lived. There could hardly
have been propounded a more revolutionary view than
this in post-exilic Israel, for it presupposed not simply
the special role of Israel with which they were familiar
already, but an equally important role for the great
nations of the world whom, up to this point, Israel had
regarded with fear and abhorrence. It is an extremely
striking feature of the book of Jonah that it is the pagans
who come out of it best. The sailors had a more practical
belief in the power and providence of God than Jonah
himself who was fast asleep amidst the turmoils of the
world, indifferent alike to God and to humanity. They
even rowed hard to save him, little though he deserved it.
Even the King of Nineveh, that hated symbol of foreign
power, 'arose from his throne, and laid his robe from him,
and covered him with sackcloth, and sat in ashes. And he
made proclamation and published through Nineveh by
the decree of the King and his nobles, saying . . . let them
turn every one from his evil way, and from the violence
that is in their hands. Who knoweth whether God will
not turn and repent, turn away from his fierce anger,
that we perish not?'

Most preachers would have been pleased indeed at the
response to so brief a sermon as Jonah's, but not Jonah –
'it displeased him exceedingly'. There could hardly be a
more biting satire than the contrast between the Hebrews'
consciousness of divine vocation and their reluctance to give
it practical expression. This is by any standards an
astonishing book, as astonishing as a book arising out of
the Jewish community in Nazi Germany proclaiming the
conviction that if only the Jews would rise to their
vocation, leave their ghettos, cast away their fear and
preach repentance at Berchtesgaden, Hitler would repent
in dust and ashes. What is even more astonishing is that
such a book, flying in the face of so much that had become
typical of Hebrew life in the post-exilic period, should have
commanded sufficient assent in Israel to retain its place in
the sacred Canon of the Prophets. It shows, I believe, the
little observed but pervasively powerful influence of the
prophetic school that a book of this kind should arise

out of it long after the period of great prophecy was believed to have ended, and that it should become part of the stock-in-trade of synagogue reading and preaching. That truth is never spoken as clearly again until it was spoken in the synagogue at Nazareth, when our Lord dared to say that, 'There were many widows in Israel in the days of Elijah, when the heaven was shut up three years and six months, when there came a great famine over all the land; and unto none of them was Elijah sent, but only to Zarephath, in the land of Sidon, unto a woman that was a widow. And there were many lepers in Israel in the time of Elisha the prophet; and none of them was cleansed, but only Naaman the Syrian.' Observe also the response to that sermon in the synagogue. 'And they were all filled with wrath in the synagogue . . . and they rose up, and cast him forth out of the city, and led him unto the brow of the hill whereon their city was built, that they might throw him down headlong.' The prophets of universal mission have always found it hard to get a hearing and never more so than in the last centuries of the pre-Christian era when the Jews, in defiance of their own Scriptures, clung doggedly to doctrines and attitudes which proved in the end to be a total misunderstanding of their distinctive role in the world.

In defiance of their own Scriptures? Was it not Ezra who rebuilt the walls of Jerusalem and more significantly built a wall of pure dogma round the Jewish people? Did not the psalmists occasionally exult in the defeat of their enemies? Did not the prophet Joel himself look forward with unedifying glee to the utter desolation of Nineveh? Did not the law of Moses itself lay upon the people such dietary laws as to separate them unmistakably from the rest of humanity? The point I would wish to make is that this only demonstrates the danger of treating the Scriptures as a series of texts unrelated to the author's intention and to the circumstances under which they were written, and then proceeding to use them in pursuit of an opinion or a dogma which these texts were never meant to uphold. The only safe way of reading the Scriptures (though in another sense it is a dangerous way) is to look at them as a whole; to perceive the main drift; to make discriminations between the less important and the more important; to observe what is eternal and what is merely temporal; to make allowances for the circumstances under which the authors wrote and the public for which they wrote. If I may use an analogy, as before, any great Cathedral will have within it certain inadequacies of workmanship, symbolic representations which are sometimes plainly disagreeable, parts of the edifice which do not relate satisfactorily to other parts, but to treat it in this piecemeal way is to miss its message. Stand in that great Cathedral with the sun pouring through the windows, observe its great arches and its sweeping vault, listen again to the voices of countless worshippers down the centuries praying their hearts out in that place, and you will know that it is indeed the Lord who reigns and who is represented in the impressive complex of wood and stone and glass.

I return to my theme – the Lord is King. Jonah was one of the few who perceived the great truth that is elsewhere enunciated in the Scriptures, though only indirectly, that if the Lord is Lord at all, he must be Lord of all. Even the kingdom of Nineveh, that harlot of the ancient world, is capable of hearing the voice of God and repenting and believing. It was the tragedy of the Judaism of the post-exilic period not that they believed in God too much but that they believed in him too little. They allowed him to become just their King; they allowed their kingdom to become just one of the kingdoms of the world. Jonah in the belly of the great fish heard a message seemingly at variance with the message Daniel received in the lions' den; both have their importance but I know the one to which I would give the priority. It is the message of Jonah summoning the Church to mission in the world.

NOTABLE PASSAGES

See page 21. Read all Jonah. Compare a similar manifesto, the Book of Ruth.

14 One foot in Eden
Genesis

You will take it as an extreme example of the author's perversity that he should reserve the first book of the Bible for the last chapter – but there is method in my madness. We tried to start with those books which could most readily be understood by someone unfamiliar with Hebrew history, Hebrew thought and Hebrew literary conventions. The book of Genesis is not a difficult book in one sense, in so far as it can be understood at one level by a child. In another sense, however, it is an extremely profound book, requiring for meaningful interpretation considerable understanding of Hebrew life and culture. It is the apogee of the writer's art, revelling in subtle nuances of style, and requiring from the reader some awareness of the theological issues which troubled the people of God in the author's time – whatever that time was. It is called in the Hebrew Bible '*Bereshit*' which is, as usual, just the opening word of the book, 'In the beginning'. That word is not meant simply as a heading to the origins of the world and creation but to the origins of the customs and institutions of Israel.

Let us assume for the moment that the author was writing in the early part of the monarchy, when the people of Israel were much aware of their tribal divisions. They had a Temple on the holy hill of Zion, with a priesthood and a sacrificial system. They were familiar with local shrines served by a local priest in the area where they happened to live; they had a Law, as the means of regulating their common life; and an elementary judicial system to which a litigant could apply; they had prophets and judges and singers and psalmists; they played out their part in a complex social system which had to take account of the other inhabitants of the land of Canaan, who worshipped other gods and lived by other laws. The government of the day had commercial relationships with Tyre and Phoenicia and with those other mixed and moving populations which inhabited the Fertile Crescent. To all intents and purposes the Hebrews were not significantly different from those amongst whom they lived; they looked like them, they spoke not altogether dissimilar languages, they married, they got sick and died; they lost their crops when the rains failed; they had their villages ravaged by casual marauders. As we have seen before, they did not live in a ghetto but were part and parcel of the ancient world, with its class structures and something that approximated to a common culture (see Appendix 4). Yet they were conscious of being different and that consciousness could be stirred by prophets like Elijah and Elisha either into a positive holy war with their neighbours or a renewed resistance to foreign customs and foreign gods. In short, for all their similarities with the surrounding races, they refused to be absorbed into and lost within Canaanite culture. If, however, their distinctiveness was to be preserved, then that distinctiveness had to be understood on the basis of that process of history by which the Hebrew nation came into existence. The book of Genesis is not just history, it is (to use the technical term) aetiological history, that is to say, a study of the origins of the distinctive institutions and the distinctive customs of the Hebrew people.

As we have seen, the books of Exodus, Leviticus and Numbers are dominated by the figure of Moses, to whom the people habitually looked back as the fountainhead of their religion, the giver of their Law, the inspirer of their Temple, the father-figure who presided over all. But whence Moses and the Red Sea and the wilderness? The latter part of the book of Genesis offers a simple answer and it is this – that Jacob, the father of the race comprising the twelve tribes, had a son Joseph who dreamed dreams and saw visions and became understandably unpopular with his brothers. Joseph was sold into Egypt where, like Daniel after him, he flourished exceedingly by reason of his skill in the interpretation of dreams. He became virtually prime minister of Egypt and by his foresight and administrative skill saved Pharaoh and his nation from the worst consequences of world-wide famine. It was thus, when the famine struck, that Jacob and the other members of his family settled in Egypt under the aegis of Joseph. Joseph, for all his 'Technicolour Dreamcoat', is not in the pages of Scripture a very colourful person, but he occupies an extremely important place in the theology of Israel: he is an example of the godly man who, in a heathen environment, preserved his faith in God and was enabled to save the church, thus demonstrating in a remarkable way the care which the God of the Universe had for this particular little group of nomads. The Joseph stories are the opening bars of a variation on a familiar theme within the Holy Scriptures – the victimisation of the just, who by the providence of God rise superior to their circumstances, triumph over their enemies and establish a succession. So we are introduced to the origins of the race and to the story of the oppression in Egypt, which led ultimately to the call of Moses and the giving of the Law (see Appendix 4).

We must not take too much account of the division of the Pentateuch into five books; bear in mind always that the heart and core of the Hebrew faith lay in their reception of the Law. Everything led up to it – everything else led away from it. Joseph acquires importance not for the vividness of his faith in God, which is not always apparent, nor for his asceticism, which is even less apparent, but for the place he happens to occupy in that providential ordering of history by which a slave people in Egypt were chosen to be the recipients and guardians of God's revelation to the world. But the life of the nation did not begin with Joseph, nor even with Jacob (who first received the name Israel); it began, so the author says, when their forefather Abraham was called by Yahweh to leave his own country and his kindred and his father's house and move to Canaan, and it is this remarkable man Abraham that we now consider.

A remarkable man? There have been persuasive voices raised to ask whether Abraham was ever an individual man and not simply the name of one of the great migratory tribes. For all the efforts to inter him, however, Abraham remains obstinately alive, and the chapters concerning him are amongst the most vivid and instructive anywhere in the Scriptures. They are not written just for the delectation of the reader, however, nor for his instruction in the ways of God with a man. The author wishes us to understand that the history of his people is to be interpreted not simply in terms of Moses or of Joseph but of their great forefather according to the flesh, Abraham; he is the origin of the chosen people, chosen no doubt much against his will to leave the cultural riches of Babylon and to become a wanderer on the face of the earth. How did it happen?

Under what circumstances did Abraham hear the call?
What God was it whose word he was hearing? The author
vouchsafes no answer to these questions because there is
no answer. There is simply the mysterious fact that a
God who identified himself as Yahweh, the Lord,
communicated effectively with Abraham in Babylon and
continued to communicate with him throughout his
wanderings thereafter. We are in the presence of the
mystery whereby God intervenes in human history and in
human lives.

Abraham's life is a life impregnated throughout with an
extraordinary sense of God's presence and God's will, for
which there is no rational explanation nor ever can be;
God speaks, and, listening, the dead receive new life.
Rationalise Abraham out if you wish, give him another
name, provide him with another history, but the life of the
Hebrew nation is inexplicable without that experience
which is repeated over and over again in the lives of
psalmist and prophet – that God speaks to men and
makes his will known.

  'Out of the stillness may be heard
    The formative, unspoken word;
  Creative, moveless, and we come
    Into the heart of silence, home.'
It is not simply Abraham of whom the author is writing
but of himself and of patient heroic souls in Israel who
looked for a city which had foundations, whose builder
and maker was God. This is the central religious factor
and without it the Bible is meaningless and, as far as I
am concerned, human existence is meaningless as well.
But as I have said, the author is not content to initiate
you into the mysteries of religion; he is using the story of
Abraham as a theological model to which in his view the
life of Israel should conform. He dares to go back
behind those institutions of law and temple and priesthood
which made Israel a peculiar people, walled in from the
world, to the more basic factors in their origins
represented by the figure of Abraham. This was a daring
thing to do. It was the appeal to Abraham which got our
Lord into trouble with the scribes of his day, because that
appeal seemed to challenge the Mosaic institutions by
which they lived.

Abraham, as St. Paul claimed in the interests of his own

position, walked by faith and not by law. He, not Moses, is the real progenitor of the Hebrew people, the founder of the Church, the instrument of God's will. Abraham was no gypsy with a handful of pegs to sell, clinging to a few wretched possessions. He was rich in the only way in which it was possible to be rich – in flocks and cattle and children and camp followers. He stood on equal terms with kings and rulers; he enjoyed personal relationships with those whom the Hebrew nation came later to abhor – with the Pharaoh in Egypt, with the Philistines (an anachronism in that context but an instructive anachronism just the same); with the King of Gerar; with the Hittites; he is even treated as an equal by that mysterious figure Melchizedek, King of Salem, priest of God Most High. David's capture of Jerusalem and his establishing worship and court there was not just a military exploit, nor a political act. In the Hebrew view he was simply making effective that which was already implicit in God's call to Abraham and in the blessing which he received from Melchizedek the priest of God Most High (Genesis ch. 14).

What a different concept of the Hebrew vocation is here envisaged – not a people behind walls, separated by slavish customs from their neighbours, but a people moving at ease and freely in the world, digging wells and letting them silt up, building altars and leaving them behind, pilgrims indeed, walking the steep paths of human existence with confidence and faith, blessed by God and a means of blessing to the nations. In a theological sense the author of Genesis could have been a contemporary of the writer of second Isaiah or of Jonah. It is the same message addressed to the same situation.

But the author's vision embraces not simply the mountains and plains of the Promised Land, nor the culture of the Fertile Crescent; it embraces the whole created universe. This is the significance of the first eleven chapters of the book. They are not, please not, intended as a guide to geology or biology, to psychiatry or to social reform, to women's lib. or to sexual freedom. These early chapters represent an analysis of human existence which was as true in the author's day as in the days of Adam; as true of us as of the inhabitants of the world in the eighth century BC. The author does not offer explanations, he simply observes. He observes the Tower of Babel and the

consequences of that persistent arrogance in mankind
which seeks in its own strength to build a tower up to
heaven. Tower blocks are no new phenomenon; they are
as old as the Ziggurats of the civilisation to which the
author of Genesis belonged. He observes the industrial
society of his day in the person of Tabul-Cain, the forger
of every cutting instrument of brass and iron; he observes
the custom of implacable revenge and the bitterness of
internecine strife between Cain and Abel; he observes the
sense of shame seemingly inescapably associated with the
sexual act; he observes with uncanny insight the source of
all our bitternesses in the desire at all costs to have our
own way, to seek our own enjoyment, to sacrifice the
good we enjoy for the good we dimly imagine.

The names Adam and Eve are not proper names: Adam
is the name for man, Eve means 'the living one'; indeed
the whole point of the story would be destroyed if they
were individual proper names. They represent the universal
experience of mankind; in every stately home of the land,
behind every cottage door and in every suburban garden
dwell an Adam and an Eve tormented with the problems
which are common to all men and women and seeking,
often in vain, salvation from them. This is our experience –
no more, no less; we have no experience of the primaeval
garden where every prospect pleases and where we have
everything we need. This is not something in the past
which we have somehow lost; this is something of the
future which we have yet to experience. And the means
by which we are to experience it? The audacity of the
author is staggering; he says that the means by which
mankind is to create a garden on the earth, where people
will live in amity and peace and have sufficient for all their
need (the environmental dream), is to be found in the
peculiar vocation of the people of Israel. Really this is
too much. But the author is saying no less; he is saying to
his contemporaries in the ninth, eighth, seventh or sixth
century BC that the institutions they observe, the people
to which they belong, are the means chosen by God
whereby the earth may be what God wills it to be, that is,
the garden of the Lord, where men and women love each
other without shame and where God walks in the cool of
the evening. It is a sublime picture and only religious
genius could ever have etched it out. In that sense at
least the book of Genesis is timeless; it is a more reliable

guide to the theology of mission than anything to be found elsewhere in the Sacred Scriptures. For the original vocation of Israel is to mission; not to sit behind Nehemiah's walls and hug Ezra's law but to move freely amongst mankind, offering salvation not only of the individual soul but of social and international life. It is never so clear again as in Genesis that the Lord who called Abraham is Lord of all, and that on obedience to him depends all human blessedness.

Edwin Muir, the great Scottish poet, remarkable for his astonishing penetration into these ancient narratives of the book of Genesis, puts it thus:

'One foot in Eden still, I stand
   And look across the other land.
The world's great day is growing late,
   Yet strange these fields that we have planted
So long with crops of love and hate.
   Time's handiworks by time are haunted,
And nothing now can separate
   The corn and tares compactly grown.
The armorial weed in stillness bound
   About the stalk; these are our own.
Evil and good stand thick around
   In the fields of charity and sin
Where we shall lead our harvest in.'

The book of Genesis fills me with great hope, when hope is generally in short supply. It fills me with great hope because one great man of God, the author of this book, looking back across the wrecks of time, haunted by his own inadequacies, bored by the brutalities and banalities of everyday existence, still holds fast to paradise. It must be so if the Lord is Lord of all.

NOTABLE PASSAGES

Genesis 6:9–22
Genesis 12:1–9

15 Jerusalem to Jericho
The end of the journey

One of the memorable experiences in an altogether
memorable study leave which I once enjoyed in Israel,
was a long-awaited walk from Jerusalem to Jericho, across
the Judaean hills, following such relics as remain of the
old Roman road. We started before dawn to avoid the
worst of the August heat and saw the sun rise in all its
glory over those bleak but beautiful hills, with the outlines
of the mountains of Moab rising in the distance on the
other side of the Dead Sea. It was an entrancing experience,
offering unexpected vistas and providing geographical
relationships between places and scenes which we otherwise
knew only in isolation from each other. But perhaps more
startling still was the awareness that we had the ground
under our feet upon which Abraham had passed with his
flocks, over which Joshua had marched his triumphant
army, in which David had hunted and fought – and over
which the weary legionaries of Rome had dragged their
siege engines for the last great siege of Jerusalem. Nothing
much had changed: the Bedouin were still in their
encampments, their dogs still barked at unwanted intruders
and the sun still shone, as it had long done, on the hard
rocks and sparse vegetation of this eroded landscape. But
then we are separated from the biblical writers by a mere
two or three thousand years, which is as nothing in the
span of human history. We must not be surprised, therefore,
to find that many of the issues in Church and community
which seem to us intensely and painfully modern, are
indistinguishable from the issues to which the writers of
the Bible addressed themselves.

The Bible appears at first sight to be a very specialised
view of history and so in one sense it is. It relates to an
extremely small section of the human race (the Hebrews
and their near neighbours), over a very restricted period
(about a thousand years), but it is like looking through a
slit window in Herod's castle at Herodium – it is a very
narrow aperture but it exposes the beholder to an
astonishing view of the world around. Or, to put it another
way, the Old Testament is a kind of paradigm or a model

sufficiently broad-based and comprehensive to provide a
standard of interpretation for all history and for all human
experience. Unlike most other religious books the Bible is
firmly embedded in history, in the rocks and shale and
soil of identifiable human experience. It is full of names, of
measurements, of dates and dynasts; the issues to which it
attends, often almost by the way, are the issues to which we
still have to attend – and that is irrespective of the fact
that we speak of nuclear deterrents rather than a sling and
a stone; that we measure things in miles or kilometres
rather than in cubits; that we look to economists rather
than to soothsayers for our expectations of the future.
'There is nothing new under the sun' our cynical friend,
the author of Ecclesiastes, said, whether it is the burning,
unrelenting sun of the Judaean hills or the pale intermittent
sun of an English winter. You may, therefore, properly
look to the Old Testament for guidance in those issues
that trouble the Church of our own day. I now suggest
a few examples which you may bear in mind as you read it.

Churchmen profess to be troubled by doubts about the
future of that great institution to which they belong and
which they serve. 'The institutional phase is over', we
say, and so it is, of course, if by that we mean that we can
no longer look for an unthinking devotion to ancient
institutions just because they are ancient, in the way we
might have done up to about the end of the last century.
This issue is never far below the surface in the Old
Testament. The bulk of the people of Israel, for the bulk
of their history, rested their faith upon the antiquity of the
institution to which they belonged. In good times and in
bad, but perhaps especially in bad times, they rested their
confidence in the divine authority of the Law, the prevailing
power of the sacrificial system and the invulnerability of
the city of Jerusalem. This was why the catastrophe of 587
was a catastrophe, for all three elements in the average
Israelite's faith were either destroyed or heavily undermined.
But for three hundred years, off and on, the great Prophets
of Israel had been preparing the people for precisely this
kind of catastrophe. They had warned the people that their
favour with God depended not on the possession of the
Law but on obedience to it; they poured scorn on the
elaborate rituals of the Temple and even went so far
sometimes as to tell the people to stay away from church;
they had predicted that the various alliances into which the

government had entered for the protection of their sacred
city were no substitute for the protection of the Living
God. So Jeremiah certainly was not surprised when
Jerusalem fell. The prophets maintained a seemingly
ambivalent but in fact perfectly logical attitude to the
great institutions of their day; they recognised their
existence, they valued them as symbols of their people's
life and they never doubted that some such institutions
were indispensable. But no human institution can claim
for itself that unambiguous authority which belongs to
God alone. The proud institutions of the world, whether
they be of the Church or of the State, come under the same
judgement as the tower which men sought to raise to
heaven. It is precisely at the moment when the secular
or sacred institutions seem at their strongest and most
enduring that they come under judgement. Ask yourself
occasionally, do you love God or do you love your
institution?

Take another example. The one great feature which
distinguished Israel from their neighbours, was their
astonishing sense of 'chosenness'. Even the documents we
have been studying fall short of any complete explanation
as to why this should have been so but they are unanimous
(and I mean unanimous) in asserting or assuming that it
was so. The people of Israel had a divine vocation and it
was not a vocation given to them by a tribal deity but by
the Lord of the whole earth. Observe, however, in the
documents (in so far as we have been able to date them
accurately) how this sense of divine vocation suffers from
a severe narrowing of perspective, until that vocation in
post-exilic Israel amounts to little more than the will to
survive. They sat in the ghettoes of the ancient world
with their wings of aspiration furled. The Pharisees did
indeed compass heaven and earth to make a single
proselyte – but was it a proselyte to their great institution
that they wanted, or a willing convert to the Living God?
So it took people of the stamp of the writer of second
Isaiah or of the book of Jonah or even more notably that
theologian responsible for the final shape of the book of
Genesis, to recall the people to their true vocation, which
was – to be a means of blessing to all nations. Look at
the Church to which you belong, huddled in its pews,
nursing its privileges, clinging to a Victorian past, uttering
its theological slogans, priding itself on its soundness or

orthodoxy; Ezra and Nehemiah live on in your midst.

Take now the idea of tradition which has played so fateful a part in the history of the Church, both Jewish and Christian. Judaism was an historical religion; by that we mean that it was bedded in history and had a history of its own. It was created by events and it was natural, therefore, to look back to those events and to the interpretation of them as the foundation of the faith. The Jews, therefore, looked back, and rightly so, to the Exodus, to the wilderness wanderings and the giving of the Law as the data of their existence as a chosen people; yet we have already seen the deadening effects of that tradition when it is dissociated from a living present experience of the God who works not only in past history but in present history. The Scribes of our Lord's day sat in Moses' seat, endlessly elaborating the tradition which they had received from their forefather, fastening the attention of their audiences on an event of the past. It is noteworthy that the prophets of the eighth and seventh centuries were not lavish in their references to the past, because they wished their audiences to see that the hand of God was at work in the present, offering new revelations of himself in the events of the contemporary world – and largely 'secular' events at that. That is why our Lord, and subsequently the great Apostle St. Paul, found it necessary to appeal back behind the Mosaic tradition to a tradition more original and universal even than that. Paul did not simply appeal to Caesar, he appealed to Abraham.

The people of Israel, however, lived not only with a national tradition, they lived with an individual one as well and the Proverbs bear witness to a crude, homespun, dogmatic view of human experience which fundamentally saw everything in simple terms – the righteous (especially the Jewish righteous) flourished and the ungodly were punished. The fact that this did not accord with everyday experience did not deter the wise men of Israel; this is what they had been taught, this is what they proposed to convey in safety to their descendants. It took someone of a sceptical turn of mind like the author of Ecclesiastes, or instinctively religious turn of mind like the author of Job, to challenge these old and unsatisfactory traditions. The message is the same as before: devotion to antiquity, however hallowed, is no substitute for an up-to-date experience of the Living God, as he is encountered in the everyday details of home life or in the wider context of international diplomacy. The name of Israel's God was 'I AM' not 'I WAS'. The pages of the Old Testament constantly reflect this age-long battle between the traditionalist and the radical. We must not shrink from that battle in our own time.

I would be doing less than justice to Jewish scholars, whom I number amongst my friends and acquaintances, if I failed to mention one other issue which may seem strangely unimportant in a world full of burning issues – I refer to the relationship between Jews and Christians. I need hardly say that this is primarily a theological and not a racial issue. This has been a book about the Old Testament and I have avoided any reference to the New Testament, except in so far as it genuinely illuminates a theology which stands on its own and is represented in the Old Testament. But in fact there is only one theology, and that is the theology of the Old Testament. Jesus, Paul and the other Apostles knew no other theology; they believed, as their predecessors in that faith believed, that the God of Israel was the God of the whole earth and the creator of the universe; that he had made his will known to a chosen people; that he desired all men everywhere to come to the knowledge of the truth and that he proposed to achieve this through his chosen representatives on earth. That is the theology of the Old Testament and that is the theology by which, whether we are Jews or Christians, we live. The New Testament does not alter that theology one whit, it simply points it up and announces that God's purpose, once seen to be effective in the life of Israel, was now to be seen as supremely effective in a particular member of that race, Jesus of Nazareth.

Christians need constantly to be recalled to the fact that Jesus was a Jew, sharing the traditions and aspirations of his people; following as far as he could their customs, suffering and rejoicing with them in the accidents of their history. The Old Testament is not abolished by the coming of Christ; it is irrevocably confirmed as a proper representation of God's nature and God's will. I have some sympathy, therefore, for those Jewish scholars who still speak of the 'separation' between Christians and Jews, as we would tend to speak of the great schism between

East and West or the division of the Western Church at
the Reformation. The use of the term 'separation' properly
suggests that we are all the children of Abraham; we
worship still the God of Abraham, Isaac and Jacob; we are
grafted into the tree which is rooted and grounded in the
soil of Palestine. There is only one Church and that is the
Church which set out from Haran to settle in the Promised
Land. St. Paul is a thorough-going critic of his own people,
as he could afford to be as a Hebrew of the Hebrews and
a Pharisee, but he never let go of the fact that the Church
of Israel and the Church of Christ were one, and that the
day would come when the ancient people of God, even
those who had long departed from orthodoxy, would be
grafted back into the one tree. This is a more important
issue than we might imagine; our theology is altogether
too Christian, insufficiently Hebrew.

It was an illuminating experience to descend from the
uplands of Judaea to the banks of the Dead Sea and the
ancient city of Jericho, to sit outside a café and drink
coca-cola, to sweat in tropical heat and be assaulted once
more with the carbon monoxide of passing traffic. So
you may feel as you descend from the uplands of Bible
study to the stupefying din and confusion of contemporary
life in your factory, your office or your down-town parish.
But that is what I believe Bible study is all about. It is
not to be regarded as a means of achieving pleasant
devotional thought or writing little sermons for yourself
or preparing homilies for the Bible Class or instructing
your congregation; it is that you may inhabit for some
time every day an upland place, where you may have a
cool wind on your face and be able to look into the
distance; where you may be alone with the God of Sinai;
where you may perceive the marchings and counter-
marchings of the armies on the plain with a greater sense
of detachment; where you may capture anew the vision of
One who rules over the world and holds the nations in the
hollow of his hand. You may be far from the uplands of
Judaea but you are no further than the bookshelf on the
other side of the room from the experience which those
uplands yielded. You may drink again at the well from
which Abraham drank; you may struggle at the stream
with the God whom Jacob encountered; you may look at
the Church to which you belong with the zeal and
compassion of the Amos who lived in those barren hills –

this in a book about mankind, for all mankind, written to glorify him who is Lord of all.

I end with a quotation from that great man of God, P. T. Forsyth: 'May He show us up there apart, transfigured things in a noble light. May He prepare us for the sorrows of the valley by a glorious peace, and for the action of life by a fellowship gracious, warm and noble. So may we face all the harsh realisms of time, in the reality, power and kindness of the eternal, whose mercy is as His majesty for ever.'

Group aids from BRF
Bible Reading Fellowship study group outlines combine
simple introductions with questions devised to point up
the teaching of Scripture and to stimulate thought about
its meaning and application for the group.

Old Testament titles:
Genesis 1–11 (S201)
Genesis 12–50 (S202)
Exodus (S203)
Amos (S204)
Jeremiah (S205)
Others to follow

FULL DETAILS FROM

BRF, St. Michael's House, 2 Elizabeth Street, London
SW1W 9RQ
or
BRF, P.O. Box M, Winter Park, Florida 32789, USA
or
BRF, Jamieson House, Constitution Avenue, Reid ACT
2601, Australia.

Questions for discussion

1. In what ways, if any, does Ecclesiastes remind you of the society in which we live? (Chapter 3)

2. Job is said to be a radical. What is a 'radical'? (Chapter 4)

3. To what extent are the Psalms:
(a) distinctively Jewish?
(b) of universal appeal? (Chapter 5)

4. '587 and all that.' What does the Old Testament have to say about our attitudes to national crisis? (Chapter 7)

5. What is the relevance of Deuteronomy to us? (Chapter 8)

6. What do the prophetic writings tell us about:
(a) the Charismatic movement?
(b) the Church's role in politics? (Chapter 9)

7. Does the Decalogue (Ten Commandments) offer a secure and practical basis for national life? (Chapter 10)

8. What is your ideal of the Church – a separated community or a community committed to public life? (Chapter 11)

9. To what extent can the Church be expected to go along with the culture of the day? (Chapter 12)

10. What is the message of Jonah for the Church to which you belong? (Chapter 13)

11. What may we deduce from Genesis about the origins and role of the people of God? (Chapter 14)

12. How, as a result of your reading, do you now understand the relationship between Jews and Christians? (Chapter 15)

Appendix 1

A Guide to Translations of the Old Testament in English

1. Authorised Version (King James)
Still unrivalled as literature but based on an old text
long since superseded. (See page 4.)

2. Revised Version (1885)
A painstaking but not very elegant attempt to correct
the Authorised Version. Still useful for study purposes.

3. A New Translation of the Bible by James Moffat
(1924)
A one-man job and all the more remarkable for that.
The first attempt to present a genuinely modern translation
in English.

4. Knox Translation (1948)
Designed (in the translator's words) 'to speak to
Englishmen not only in English words but in English
idiom'. It was intended for use amongst Roman Catholics
and is based on the Vulgate.

5. Revised Standard Version (1952)
A revision, as the title suggests, not a new translation,
which does improve considerably on the Revised Version.
The 'Teachers' Edition' is particularly useful. This version
also features in the *Oxford Annotated Bible*.

6. Soncino Bible (1958 – 14 volumes)
Primarily intended for Jewish readers, with Hebrew text
and English translation and verse-by-verse commentary.

7. Four Prophets (J. B. Phillips 1963)
A new translation of Amos, Hosea, Isaiah and Micah, and
a valuable introduction to the Prophets as a whole.

8. Jerusalem Bible (1966)
So-called because it is based on a text by the Dominican

Biblical School in Jerusalem. The translation itself and
the explanatory notes are excellent.

9. Jerusalem Bible (1969)
Not to be confused with the above. It is intended for
Jewish readers with the Hebrew text on one side and the
English translation on the other. The English is traditional
in style.

10. New English Bible (1970)
The most authoritative of the new translations and widely
accepted in the English-speaking world. Aim for the
edition which includes the 'Concise Readers' Guide'.

11. Living Bible (1971)
An astonishing achievement for one man. It does not
claim to be an exact translation (and is not) but it certainly
brings the Scriptures to life.

12. Today's English Version
The sections so far published augur well for the complete
work. It is based on a sound text and is genuinely 'for
today'.

13. The Bible in Order (1975)
This is the first attempt ever made to arrange the books
of the Bible in the order in which they were written or
edited – an extremely useful tool for Bible study. It is
expensive, but every library may be expected to have a copy.

Appendix 2

THE HEBREW CANON OF OLD TESTAMENT

A. The Torah
Genesis
Exodus
Leviticus
Numbers
Deuteronomy

B. The Prophets
Joshua
Judges
Samuel
Kings
} 1. *Former*

Isaiah
Jeremiah
Ezekiel
The Twelve Prophets
} 2. *Latter*

C. The Holy Writings
Psalms
Proverbs
Job
Song of Songs
Ruth
Lamentations
Ecclesiastes
Esther
Daniel
Ezra – Nehemiah
Chronicles

Appendix 3

A Chart of Old Testament History and Literature
The purpose of the chart is to help the reader by
co-ordinating the history and the literature. It is not possible
to be precise about the dates of the literature, nor does a
suggested date rule out the possibility of additions to
completed books (as evidenced by the additions to Daniel
and Esther in the Greek versions).

* approximate dates

1. The Patriarchal Age (2000*–
   1300* BC)

2. The Age of Moses, Joshua,   Judges ch. 5 1100*
   and Judges (1300*–1000* BC)

3. Samuel, Saul, David and   Oldest of the Psalms and other
   Solomon (1050–931)   poetry 1200–950*

4. Pre-exilic Period (931–587)   Oldest prose parts (J?) of the
                                     Pentateuch (950–850)
   a. The Divided Monarchy   Amos 760–750*
   b. The Assyrian Destruction of   Hosea 745–725*
      the Northern Kingdom   Isaiah 740–701*
      722/721   Early prose parts of Joshua-
                                     Judges-Samuel-Kings 800–700*
                                     Micah 725–690*
   c. Reign of Josiah 640–609   Zephaniah 630–625*
                                     Habakkuk 625–600*
                                     First edition of Deuteronomy
                                     and deuteronomic writings
   d. The Fall of Assyrian   Nahum 612–610*
      Nineveh to the Babylonians   Jeremiah 626–586*
      612 BC
   e. The Babylonian Invasion of
      Judah 598
   f. Destruction of Judah and
      the Exile to Babylonia 587

5. The Exilic Period (587–539)

    a. The Persian conquest of Babylonia 539
    b. The Return from Exile 539*–516

Passages in Jeremiah
Ezekiel 593*–560*
Second Isaiah (chs. 40–55) 539–520*
Further compilation of elements in Pentateuch

6. The Post-Exilic Period (530*–167)
    a. Persian Period 538–333
    b. Careers of Ezra and Nehemiah 450*

Haggai 520
Zechariah 520–518

Malachi, Joel (?), Obadiah 500–450*
Third Isaiah (?) 500–450
Priestly completion of the Pentateuch 450–400*
Compilation of Proverbs 400*
Job 450–350* (or possibly earlier)
Jonah, Ruth 425*
Ezra-Nehemiah-Chronicles 375–250*

    c. Greek Period 333–167

Possible final compilation of prophetic books
Ecclesiastes 375–350*
Translation of the Pentateuch into Greek 250*

7. Maccabean Period (167–63 BC)

Daniel 166–165*

8. Roman Period (63 BC–5th century AD)
Destruction of Temple in Jerusalem AD 70

Appendix 4

A chart of World History Contemporary with the Biblical period

* approximate date. All dates (in bold) are BC

History	Literature
2000*Bronze Age in Britain and Northern Europe	**2000***Egyptians developed a quasi-alphabet of 24 consonants
1925*The Hittites attacked and plundered Babylon	**1925***Ugaritic cuneiform writing
1850	**1850***Beginnings of Semitic alphabet
1800*Hammurabi of Babylon set laws of kingdom in order	
1750 Beginnings of Persian Empire (to *550 BC)	
1700*Disturbances in Asia Minor began to threaten the prosperity of Egypt	
1650 Egyptians driven south by Asiatic refugees known as the Hyksos, who formed a kingdom in the Nile Delta	
1575 Ahmosis, first king of new Egyptian dynasty, defeated and expelled by Hyksos, who were forced back into Syria and Canaan	
1500*Peak of Canaanite civilisation in Palestine	**1500***Hymns of the *Rig Veda* composed; Upanishad tradition of Hindus (to 1000 BC)

Arts	Science

Arts

2000*City of Babylon, capital of empire
Palaces of this date have been excavated at Ugarit, in Syria

1925*Erection of great temple of Dagon and palace, at Mari

1800*Early period of development of Stonehenge; main construction 1600–1400 BC

History	Literature

1475

1400

1370 Amenhotep IV destroyed old gods of Egypt and set up worship of one god only, Aten, the Sun God

1313

1300*Regulations concerning beer-shops in Egypt

1225*Exodus of Israelites, under Moses, from Egypt

1200*The Hebrews occupied Canaan

1193 Destruction of Troy

1175 Egypt attacked and invaded; developed into two kingdoms, Upper and Lower Egypt, centred on the Delta and at Thebes

1100*Assyrian Empire began in Mesopotamia

1100*First Chinese dictionary published; contained 40,000 characters

1000*Israelite kingdom set up by David and Solomon; extended from Euphrates to Egypt by 900 BC

1000*A Hebrew alphabet developed from earlier Semitic alphabet

931*Division of Hebrew kingdom into Israel and Judah

Arts

1475*Cleopatra's Needle, so-called; an obelisk of the reign of Thutmosis III

1352*Tomb of Tut-ankh-Amun begun

Science

1400*Iron tools, including ploughshares, in use in India

1313*Aqueducts and reservoirs used for irrigation in Egypt

1200*Rise of Phoenician power in sea-trading in Mediterranean

1100*Tin mined in England; imported by Phoenicians

History	Literature

900 *Damascus strongest kingdom along the western coast of Asia *New capital, Samaria, first settled by Omri

854 War between Damascus and Assyria

850

800

781

776

753 Foundation of City of Rome

732 Damascus overthrown by Assyria

722 Sargon II of Assyria captured Samaria; kingdom of Israel ended

721

701 Sennacherib, successor of Sargon II, invaded Judah; invasion failed

Sennacherib settled Assyrian capital at Nineveh

689 Assyrians destroyed Babylon and turned the Euphrates to flow over place where city had stood

682 Submission of Hebrew kingdom of Judah to Assyria

Arts	Science
850*The Moabite Stone, in Phoenician script, erected	850*First reference, in the *Odyssey*, to use of drugs for dulling consciousness; and in the *Iliad* to diving for oysters
800*Earliest recorded music: a hymn on a Sumerian tablet	
	781 Eclipse recorded by Chinese
776 First recorded Olympic Games, possibly dating from *1350 BC; lasted intermittently for 1000 years	
	721 Electrum staters of Lydia made; possibly world's earliest coins
700*Hezekiah's water-tunnel at Jerusalem	701*Phoenicians believed to have circumnavigated Africa

History

Literature

670 Assyrians destroyed Memphis and Thebes but failed to hold Egypt

650

626 Chaldean general Nabopolassar seized Babylonian throne; declared independence from Assyria

621

612 Medes, allied with Babylonians and Scythians, destroyed Nineveh; end of Assyrian empire

606 Nebuchadnezzar made Judah tributary

600 Assyrian empire divided among its conquerors

597 First punitive attack on Jerusalem by Babylonians; leaders taken into exile

587 Nebuchadnezzar destroyed Jerusalem; 'the Exile' began

581

543 Siddhartha Gautama left home to devote himself to philosophy and asceticism

539 Cyrus II conquered Babylonia; Judah a Persian province until 333 BC

621*The Laws of Dracon; first written laws of Athens; noted for harshness

600*Beginning of second period of Chinese literature

539*Public libraries in use in Athens

Arts	Literature	Science	History
Arts		**Science**	
670*Assyrians rebuilt city of Babylon in effort to placate Babylonians			
		650*Iron came into general use in Egypt	
		600*Earliest known period for windmills (used in Persian corn-grinding)	
		581*Pythagoras, great philosopher and mathematician	

History	Science	Literature

539 Edict of Cyrus: the Return – some Jewish exiles returned to Judah

530*Gautama, now a (or the) Buddha ('Enlightened One') preached first sermon at Benares

525

525*Aeschylus, Greek tragic dramatist

522 Darius, successor to Cambyses of Persia, divided Persian empire into 20 provinces or satrapies

510 Rome declared a republic

500

490 Persian armies defeated by Greeks at Marathon

484

480

480*Euripides, Greek tragic dramatist; also Sophocles

470 Death of Confucius

460 Athens controlled by Pericles

447

445

433 (?) Nehemiah's second visit to Jerusalem

431 Peloponnesian War between Athens and Sparta began; lasted till 404 BC

Arts	Science

537 Jews began rebuilding of the Temple

510*Theatre at Delphi constructed

500*Hindus familiar with plastic surgery

484*Herodotus, Greek historian

470*Rapid development in technology and agriculture in China

460 Hippocrates, Greek physician, later seen as the ideal

447 Foundations of the Parthenon laid at Athens

445*Nehemiah rebuilt the walls of Jerusalem; opposed by Samaritans

History	Literature
429	**429** Plato, widely travelled Athenian philosopher, disciple of Socrates, born
423	**423** Aristophanes (448–380 BC): *The Clouds*, Greek satirical comedy
400	**400***Hebrew traditions collected in the Priestly Code
399	**399** Socrates accused of teachings contrary to established beliefs, condemned to death
367	
359 Philip of Macedon became King of Macedonia	
356	
350*Revolt of the Jews against Artaxerxes III of Persia; suppressed	
340	**340** Epicurus, Greek philosopher, born
338	
334 Alexander defeated Persians at Granicus	
333 Jerusalem submitted to Alexander; Palestine under Greek influence till 63 BC	
Alexander recognised Samaritan High Priesthood	
331 Babylon submitted to Alexander	

Arts   Science

429 Spartans used chemical
smoke in warfare

400*Use of catapult as weapon of
war

367 Aristotle (384–322 BC),
Greek philosopher, joined Plato
at Athens and remained at
Academy for 20 years

356 Temple of Diana at Ephesus
destroyed by fire; rebuilt soon
afterwards

338*Romans began to use coins

332 Port of Alexandria founded
by Alexander

History	Literature
326 Alexander's campaign in Punjab extended his empire to River Indus	
320 Colonies of Jews settled in Egypt and Cyrene for commercial purposes	
314 Palestine subject to Seleucid rule of Syria	
293	
287	
279	
255	**255** Beginning of the Septuagint, a Greek version of the Old Testament
250 Invasion of Britain by La Tene Iron Age people	**250***Samaritan text of the Pentateuch Parchment made at Pergamum
239	
218 Hannibal invaded Italy from north	
202	
200	**200***The *Mahabharata*, ancient Hindu poem
198 Antiochus III of Syria took Palestine from Egypt	
175 Reign of Antiochus III; Antiochus IV (Epiphanes) began; policy of Hellenisation	

Arts   **Science**

320 Alexandria became centre
of Greek learning

293*Herophilus dissected human
body and distinguished veins and
arteries

287 Archimedes, early 'applied
mathematician', born

279*Aristarchus of Samos
believed the Sun to be larger than
the earth; first suggested that the
latter rotated about former.

239 Leap year introduced into
calendar by Egyptians

202*Confucianism and Taoism
adopted as Chinese way of life
during the Han dynasty

200*Use of gears led to invention
of ox-driven water-wheel for
irrigation

175 Construction of earliest
Roman pavement

History

Literature

174

168 Persecution of the Jews by Antiochus IV

167 Maccabean revolt against Antiochus IV to defend Jewish religion

160 Judas Maccabaeus died; succeeded by Jonathan Maccabaeus

Hasmonaean line of priestly rulers established

153 Independence of Jews (till 63 BC)

143 Jonathan Maccabaeus murdered; succeeded by Simon

133 Asia Minor made into province of Rome, now ruler of main countries round Mediterranean, except Egypt

121

112*Rise of Pharisees and Sadducees

105

90 Civil war in Rome between Marius and Sulla

70

70 Birth of Virgil, great Roman poet

Arts

174 Temple of Zeus, Athens
(later completed by Hadrian)

168 Desecration of Temple at
Jerusalem by Antiochus IV

165 Temple at Jerusalem
rededicated

Science

153 First month of Roman year
changed from March to January

121*Early use of concrete in
Temple of Concord, Rome

112*Posidonius observed
relationship between tides and the
moon

105*Heron developed a School
of Mechanics and Surveying at
Alexandria; very early form of
College of Technology

History	Literature
69 Dynastic war in Palestine; Hyrcanus II deposed; rise of House of Antipater	
65 Pompey entered Syria; conquest of Palestine complete by 63 BC; Palestine now part of Roman province of Syria	
63 Pompey captured Jerusalem	
60	**60** Caesar created *Acta Diurna*, daily bulletin, forerunner of newspaper
55 North Gaul conquered by Caesar; punitive expeditions sent to Britain	
54	
50	
40 Herod, at Rome, appointed king of Judaea	
37 Herod captured Jerusalem	
34	
20	
18 Adultery made an offence against State of Rome	
6 Judaea annexed by Rome	
Birth of Jesus Christ, at Bethlehem	

Arts   **Science**

63 Marcus Tullius Tiro of Rome
invented system of shorthand (in
use for over 600 years)

54 Crassus plundered Temple
at Jerusalem

50 Early form of oboe known

34*Oldest known computer
constructed; made of bronze
(recovered 1953 from wreck of
Greek ship)

20 Herod began rebuilding
Temple at Jerusalem

History

4 Death of Herod; his territory divided among his sons

Dates from here are AD

6 Judaea became Roman province

27 Baptism and ministry of Christ

30 Crucifixion of Christ (possibly 29)

32 (?) Conversion of Saul of Tarsus; baptised and known as Paul

40

43 Roman invasion of Britain under Aulus Plautius

51

64 Ss Peter and Paul martyred at Rome

65

68 Suicide of Nero

70 Revolt of Jews against Rome; Jerusalem captured and destroyed under Titus

Constitution of rabbinic schools in Galilee

Literature

51*St. Paul believed to have written Epistle to the Galatians

65*Gospel according to Mark

Arts   **Science**

40*Church founded at Corinth;
one of earliest Christian houses

43 London believed to have
been founded by this date

Bible reading for all

The Bible Reading Fellowship links together people in 65 countries in the practice of daily Bible reading and prayer. Carefully planned booklets provide a systematic programme of reading which covers the whole Bible in 5 years. The teaching of Scripture given is always related to the life and faith of the reader and each day provides a prayer or meditation. Special note is taken of church seasons and major holy days.

Four series of dated Daily Notes are published:

Series A   For adults with some knowledge of the Bible.

Series B   For adults who are beginning daily Bible reading or who want a small booklet with the Bible passages printed, a devotional commentary and some prayers for daily use.

Compass   For junior children, with illustrations and activities.

Discovery   For young adults who want to include the Bible in their search for meaning and identity.

In each series of Notes there are questions for group discussion. These are linked with the daily readings and are used by groups of BRF members all over the world. Further aids for groups are available; some are listed on page 92.